INTRODUCTION

HISTORICAL AND CRITICAL

CHAPTER I.

OF THE SCIENCE OF GRAMMAR.

"Hæc de Grammatica quam brevissime potui: non ut omnia dicerem sectatus, (quod infinitum erat,) sed ut maxima necessaria."—QUINTILIAN. *De Inst. Orat.*, Lib. i, Cap. x.

1. Language, in the proper sense of the term, is peculiar to man; so that, without a miraculous assumption of human powers, none but human beings can make words the vehicle of thought. An imitation of some of the articulate sounds employed in speech, may be exhibited by parrots, and sometimes by domesticated ravens, and we know that almost all brute animals have their peculiar natural voices, by which they indicate their feelings, whether pleasing or painful. But *language* is an attribute of reason, and differs essentially not only from all brute voices, but even from all the chattering, jabbering, and babbling of our own species, in which there is not an intelligible meaning, with division of thought, and distinction of words.

2. Speech results from the joint exercise of the best and noblest faculties of human nature, from our rational understanding and our social affection;

and is, in the proper use of it, the peculiar ornament and distinction of man, whether we compare him with other orders in the creation, or view him as an individual preëminent among his fellows. Hence that science which makes known the nature and structure of speech, and immediately concerns the correct and elegant use of language, while it surpasses all the conceptions of the stupid or unlearned, and presents nothing that can seem desirable to the sensual and grovelling, has an intrinsic dignity which highly commends it to all persons of sense and taste, and makes it most a favourite with the most gifted minds. That science is Grammar. And though there be some geniuses who affect to despise the trammels of grammar rules, to whom it must be conceded that many things which have been unskillfully taught as such, deserve to be despised; yet it is true, as Dr. Adam remarks, that, "The study of Grammar has been considered an object of great importance by the wisest men in all ages."—*Preface to Latin and English Gram.*, p. iii.

3. Grammar bears to language several different relations, and acquires from each a nature leading to a different definition. *First,* It is to language, as knowledge is to the thing known; and as doctrine, to the truths it inculcates. In these relations, grammar is a science. It is the first of what have been called the seven sciences, or liberal branches of knowledge; namely, grammar, logic, rhetoric, arithmetic, geometry, astronomy, and music. *Secondly,* It is as skill, to the thing to be done; and as power, to the instruments it employs. In these relations, grammar is an art; and as such, has long been defined, "*ars rectè scribendi, rectèque loquendi*" the art of writing and speaking correctly. *Thirdly,* It is as navigation, to the ocean, which nautic skill alone enables men to traverse. In this relation, theory and practice combine, and grammar becomes, like navigation, a practical science. *Fourthly,* It is as a chart, to a coast which we would visit. In this relation, our grammar is a text-book, which we take as a guide, or use as a help to our own observation. *Fifthly,* It is as a single voyage, to the open

sea, the highway of nations. Such is our meaning, when we speak of the grammar of a particular text or passage.

4. Again: Grammar is to language a sort of self-examination. It turns the faculty of speech or writing upon itself for its own elucidation; and makes the tongue or the pen explain the uses and abuses to which both are liable, as well as the nature and excellency of that power, of which, these are the two grand instruments. From this account, some may begin to think that in treating of grammar we are dealing with something too various and changeable for the understanding to grasp; a dodging Proteus of the imagination, who is ever ready to assume some new shape, and elude the vigilance of the inquirer. But let the reader or student do his part; and, if he please, follow us with attention. We will endeavour, with welded links, to bind this Proteus, in such a manner that he shall neither escape from our hold, nor fail to give to the consulter an intelligible and satisfactory response. Be not discouraged, generous youth. Hark to that sweet far-reaching note:

"Sed, quanto ille magis formas se vertet in omnes,
Tanto, nate, magis contende tenacia vincla."
VIRGIL. Geor. IV, 411.

"But thou, the more he varies forms, beware
To strain his fetters with a stricter care."
DRYDEN'S VIRGIL.

5. If for a moment we consider the good and the evil that are done in the world through the medium of speech, we shall with one voice acknowledge, that not only the faculty itself, but also the manner in which it is used, is of incalculable importance to the welfare of man. But this reflection does not directly enhance our respect for grammar, because it is not to language as the vehicle of moral or of immoral sentiment, of good or of evil to mankind,

that the attention of the grammarian is particularly directed. A consideration of the subject in these relations, pertains rather to the moral philosopher. Nor are the arts of logic and rhetoric now considered to be properly within the grammarian's province. Modern science assigns to these their separate places, and restricts grammar, which at one period embraced all learning, to the knowledge of language, as respects its fitness to be the vehicle of any particular thought or sentiment which the speaker or writer may wish to convey by it. Accordingly grammar is commonly defined, by writers upon the subject, in the special sense of an art—"the *art* of speaking or writing a language with propriety or correctness."—*Webster's Dict.*

6. Lily says, "Grammatica est rectè scribendi atque loquendi ars;" that is, "Grammar is the art of writing and speaking correctly." Despauter, too, in his definition, which is quoted in a preceding paragraph, not improperly placed writing first, as being that with which grammar is primarily concerned. For it ought to be remembered, that over any fugitive colloquial dialect, which has never been fixed by visible signs, grammar has no control; and that the speaking which the art or science of grammar teaches, is exclusively that which has reference to a knowledge of letters. It is the certain tendency of writing, to improve speech. And in proportion as books are multiplied, and the knowledge of written language is diffused, local dialects, which are beneath the dignity of grammar, will always be found to grow fewer, and their differences less. There are, in the various parts of the world, many languages to which the art of grammar has never yet been applied; and to which, therefore, the definition or true idea of grammar, however general, does not properly extend. And even where it has been applied, and is now honoured as a popular branch of study, there is yet great room for improvement: barbarisms and solecisms have not been rebuked away as they deserve to be.

7. Melancthon says, "Grammatica est certa loquendi ac scribendi ratio, Latinis Latinè." Vossius, "Ars benè loquendi eóque et scribendi, atque id Latinis Latinè." Dr. Prat, "*Grammatica est rectè loquendi atque scribendi ars.*" Ruddiman also, in his Institutes of Latin Grammar, reversed the terms *writing* and *speaking*, and defined grammar, "*ars recè loquendi scribendique*;" and, either from mere imitation, or from the general observation that speech precedes writing, this arrangement of the words has been followed by most modern grammarians. Dr. Lowth embraces both terms in a more general one, and says, "Grammar is the art of *rightly expressing* our thoughts by words." It is, however, the province of grammar, to guide us not merely in the expression of our own thoughts, but also in our apprehension of the thoughts, and our interpretation of the words, of others. Hence, Perizonius, in commenting upon Sanctius's imperfect definition, "*Grammatica est ars rectè loquendi*," not improperly asks, "*et quidni intelligendi et explicandi*?" "and why not also of understanding and explaining?" Hence, too, the art of *reading* is virtually a part of grammar; for it is but the art of understanding and speaking correctly that which we have before us on paper. And Nugent has accordingly given us the following definition: "Grammar is the art of reading, speaking, and writing a language by rules."—*Introduction to Dict.*, p. xii.[1]

8. The word *rectè*, rightly, truly, correctly, which occurs in most of the foregoing Latin definitions, is censured by the learned Richard Johnson, in his Grammatical Commentaries, on account of the vagueness of its meaning. He says, it is not only ambiguous by reason of its different uses in the Latin classics, but destitute of any signification proper to grammar. But even if this be true as regards its earlier application, it may well be questioned, whether by frequency of use it has not acquired a signification which makes it proper at the present time. The English word *correctly* seems to be less liable to such an objection; and either this brief term, or some other of like import, (as, "with correctness"—"with propriety,") is still

usually employed to tell what grammar is. But can a boy learn by such means what it is, *to speak and write grammatically*? In one sense, he can; and in an other, he cannot. He may derive, from any of these terms, some idea of grammar as distinguished from other arts; but no simple definition of this, or of any other art, can communicate to him that learns it, the skill of an artist.

9. R. Johnson speaks at large of *the relation* of words to each other in sentences, as constituting in his view the most essential part of grammar; and as being a point very much overlooked, or very badly explained, by grammarians in general. His censure is just. And it seems to be as applicable to nearly all the grammars now in use, as to those which he criticised a hundred and thirty years ago. But perhaps he gives to the relation of words, (which is merely their dependence on other words according to the sense,) an earlier introduction and a more prominent place, than it ought to have in a general system of grammar. To the right use of language, he makes four things to be necessary. In citing these, I vary the language, but not the substance or the order of his positions. *First,* That we should speak and write words according to the significations which belong to them: the teaching of which now pertains to lexicography, and not to grammar, except incidentally. "*Secondly,* That we should observe *the relations* that words have one to another in sentences, and represent those relations by such variations, and particles, as are usual with authors in that language." *Thirdly,* That we should acquire a knowledge of the proper sounds of the letters, and pay a due regard to accent in pronunciation. *Fourthly,* That we should learn to write words with their proper letters, spelling them as literary men generally do.

10. From these positions, (though he sets aside the first, as pertaining to lexicography, and not now to grammar, as it formerly did,) the learned critic deduces first his four parts of the subject, and then his definition of

grammar. "Hence," says he, "there arise Four Parts of Grammar; *Analogy*, which treats of the several parts of speech, their definitions, accidents, and formations; *Syntax*, which treats of the use of those things in construction, according to their relations; *Orthography*, which treats of spelling; and *Prosody*, which treats of accenting in pronunciation. So, then, the true definition of Grammar is this: Grammar is the art of *expressing the relations* of things in construction, with due accent in speaking, and orthography in writing, according to the custom of those whose language we learn." Again he adds: "The word *relation* has other senses, taken by itself; but yet the *relation of words one to another in a sentence*, has no other signification than what I intend by it, namely, of cause, effect, means, end, manner, instrument, object, adjunct, and the like; which are names given by logicians to those relations under which the mind comprehends things, and therefore the most proper words to explain them to others. And if such things are too hard for children, then grammar is too hard; for there neither is, nor can be, any grammar without them. And a little experience will satisfy any man, that the young will as easily apprehend them, as *gender, number, declension,* and other grammar-terms." See *R. Johnson's Grammatical Commentaries*, p. 4.

11. It is true, that the *relation of words*—by which I mean that connexion between them, which the train of thought forms and suggests—or that dependence which one word has on an other according to the sense—lies at the foundation of all syntax. No rule or principle of construction can ever have any applicability beyond the limits, or contrary to the order, of this relation. To see what it is in any given case, is but to understand the meaning of the phrase or sentence. And it is plain, that no word ever necessarily agrees with an other, with which it is not thus connected in the mind of him who uses it. No word ever governs an other, to which the sense does not direct it. No word is ever required to stand immediately before or after an other, to which it has not some relation according to the meaning of

the passage. Here then are the relation, agreement, government, and arrangement, of words in sentences; and these make up the whole of syntax—but not the whole of grammar. To this one part of grammar, therefore, the relation of words is central and fundamental; and in the other parts also, there are some things to which the consideration of it is incidental; but there are many more, like spelling, pronunciation, derivation, and whatsoever belongs merely to letters, syllables, and the forms of words, with which it has, in fact, no connexion. The relation of words, therefore, should be clearly and fully explained in its proper place, under the head of syntax; but the general idea of grammar will not be brought nearer to truth, by making it to be "the art of *expressing the relations* of things in construction," &c., according to the foregoing definition.

12. The term *grammar* is derived from the Greek word [Greek: gramma], a letter. The art or science to which this term is applied, had its origin, not in cursory speech, but in the practice of writing; and speech, which is first in the order of nature, is last with reference to grammar. The matter or common subject of grammar, is language in general; which, being of two kinds, *spoken* and *written*, consists of certain combinations either of sounds or of visible signs, employed for the expression of thought. Letters and sounds, though often heedlessly confounded in the definitions given of vowels, consonants, &c., are, in their own nature, very different things. They address themselves to different senses; the former, to the sight; the latter, to the hearing. Yet, by a peculiar relation arbitrarily established between them, and in consequence of an almost endless variety in the combinations of either, they coincide in a most admirable manner, to effect the great object for which language was bestowed or invented; namely, to furnish a sure medium for the communication of thought, and the preservation of knowledge.

13. All languages, however different, have many things in common. There are points of a philosophical character, which result alike from the analysis of any language, and are founded on the very nature of human thought, and that of the sounds or other signs which are used to express it. When such principles alone are taken as the subject of inquiry, and are treated, as they sometimes have been, without regard to any of the idioms of particular languages, they constitute what is called General, Philosophical, or Universal Grammar. But to teach, with Lindley Murray and some others, that "Grammar may be considered as *consisting of two species*, Universal and Particular," and that the latter merely "applies those general principles to a particular language," is to adopt a twofold absurdity at the outset.[2] For every cultivated language has its particular grammar, in which whatsoever is universal, is necessarily included; but of which, universal or general principles form only a part, and that comparatively small. We find therefore in grammar no "two species" of the same genus; nor is the science or art, as commonly defined and understood, susceptible of division into any proper and distinct sorts, except with reference to different languages—as when we speak of Greek, Latin, French, or English grammar.

14. There is, however, as I have suggested, a certain science or philosophy of language, which has been denominated Universal Grammar; being made up of those points only, in which many or all of the different languages preserved in books, are found to coincide. All speculative minds are fond of generalization; and, in the vastness of the views which may thus be taken of grammar, such may find an entertainment which they never felt in merely learning to speak and write grammatically. But the pleasure of such contemplations is not the earliest or the most important fruit of the study. The first thing is, to know and understand the grammatical construction of our own language. Many may profit by this acquisition, who extend not their inquiries to the analogies or the idioms of other tongues. It is true, that every item of grammatical doctrine is the more worthy to be

known and regarded, in proportion as it approaches to universality. But the principles of all practical grammar, whether universal or particular, common or peculiar, must first be learned in their application to some one language, before they can be distinguished into such classes; and it is manifest, both from reason and from experience, that the youth of any nation not destitute of a good book for the purpose, may best acquire a knowledge of those principles, from the grammatical study of their native tongue.

15. Universal or Philosophical Grammar is a large field for speculation and inquiry, and embraces many things which, though true enough in themselves, are unfit to be incorporated with any system of practical grammar, however comprehensive its plan. Many authors have erred here. With what is merely theoretical, such a system should have little to do. Philosophy, dealing in generalities, resolves speech not only as a whole into its constituent parts and separable elements, as anatomy shows the use and adaptation of the parts and joints of the human body; but also as a composite into its matter and form, as one may contemplate that same body in its entireness, yet as consisting of materials, some solid and some fluid, and these curiously modelled to a particular figure. Grammar, properly so called, requires only the former of these analyses; and in conducting the same, it descends to the thousand minute particulars which are necessary to be known in practice. Nor are such things to be despised as trivial and low: ignorance of what is common and elementary, is but the more disgraceful for being ignorance of mere rudiments. "Wherefore," says Quintilian, "they are little to be respected, who represent this art as mean and barren; in which, unless you faithfully lay the foundation for the future orator, whatever superstructure you raise will tumble into ruins. It is an art, necessary to the young, pleasant to the old, the sweet companion of the retired, and one which in reference to every kind of study has in itself more of utility than of show. Let no one therefore despise as inconsiderable the

elements of grammar. Not because it is a great thing, to distinguish consonants from vowels, and afterwards divide them into semivowels and mutes; but because, to those who enter the interior parts of this temple of science, there will appear in many things a great subtilty, which is fit not only to sharpen the wits of youth, but also to exercise the loftiest erudition and science."—*De Institutione Oratoria,* Lib. i, Cap. iv.

16. Again, of the arts which spring from the composition of language. Here the art of logic, aiming solely at conviction, addresses the understanding with cool deductions of unvarnished truth; rhetoric, designing to move, in some particular direction, both the judgement and the sympathies of men, applies itself to the affections in order to persuade; and poetry, various in its character and tendency, solicits the imagination, with a view to delight, and in general also to instruct. But grammar, though intimately connected with all these, and essential to them in practice, is still too distinct from each to be identified with any of them. In regard to dignity and interest, these higher studies seem to have greatly the advantage over particular grammar; but who is willing to be an ungrammatical poet, orator, or logician? For him I do not write. But I would persuade my readers, that an acquaintance with that grammar which respects the genius of their vernacular tongue, is of primary importance to all who would cultivate a literary taste, and is a necessary introduction to the study of other languages. And it may here be observed, for the encouragement of the student, that as grammar is essentially the same thing in all languages, he who has well mastered that of his own, has overcome more than half the difficulty of learning another; and he whose knowledge of words is the most extensive, has the fewest obstacles to encounter in proceeding further.

17. It was the "original design" of grammar, says Dr. Adam, to facilitate "the acquisition of languages;" and, of all practical treatises on the subject, this is still the main purpose. In those books which are to prepare the learner

to translate from one tongue into another, seldom is any thing else attempted. In those also which profess to explain the right use of vernacular speech, must the same purpose be ever paramount, and the "original design" be kept in view. But the grammarian may teach many things incidentally. One cannot learn a language, without learning at the same time a great many opinions, facts, and principles, of some kind or other, which are necessarily embodied in it. For all language proceeds from, and is addressed to, the understanding; and he that perceives not the meaning of what he reads, makes no acquisition even of the language itself. To the science of grammar, the *nature of the ideas* conveyed by casual examples, is not very essential: to the learner, it is highly important. The best thoughts in the best diction should furnish the models for youthful study and imitation; because such language is not only the most worthy to be remembered, but the most easy to be understood. A distinction is also to be made between use and abuse. In nonsense, absurdity, or falsehood, there can never be any grammatical authority; because, however language may be abused, the usage which gives law to speech, is still that usage which is founded upon the *common sense* of mankind.

18. Grammar appeals to reason, as well as to authority, but to what extent it should do so, has been matter of dispute. "The knowledge of useful arts," says Sanctius, "is not an invention of human ingenuity, but an emanation from the Deity, descending from above for the use of man, as Minerva sprung from the brain of Jupiter. Wherefore, unless thou give thyself wholly to laborious research into the nature of things, and diligently examine the *causes and reasons* of the art thou teachest, believe me, thou shalt but see with other men's eyes, and hear with other men's ears. But the minds of many are preoccupied with a certain perverse opinion, or rather ignorant conceit, that in grammar, or the art of speaking, there are no causes, and that reason is scarcely to be appealed to for any thing;—than which idle notion, I know of nothing more foolish;—nothing can be thought of which is more

offensive. Shall man, endowed with reason, do, say, or contrive any thing, without design, and without understanding? Hear the philosophers; who positively declare that nothing comes to pass without a cause. Hear Plato himself; who affirms that names and words subsist by nature, and contends that language is derived from nature, and not from art."

19. "I know," says he, "that the Aristotelians think otherwise; but no one will doubt that names are the signs, and as it were the instruments, of things. But the instrument of any art is so adapted to that art, that for any other purpose it must seem unfit; thus with an auger we bore, and with a saw we cut wood; but we split stones with wedges, and wedges are driven with heavy mauls. We cannot therefore but believe that those who first gave names to things, did it with design; and this, I imagine, Aristotle himself understood when he said, *ad placitum nomina significare.* For those who contend that names were made by chance, are no less audacious than if they would endeavour to persuade us, that the whole order of the universe was framed together fortuitously."

20. "You will see," continues he, "that in the first language, whatever it was, the names of things were taken from Nature herself; but, though I cannot affirm this to have been the case in other tongues, yet I can easily persuade myself that in every tongue a reason can be rendered for the application of every name; and that this reason, though it is in many cases obscure, is nevertheless worthy of investigation. Many things which were not known to the earlier philosophers, were brought to light by Plato; after the death of Plato, many were discovered by Aristotle; and Aristotle was ignorant of many which are now everywhere known. For truth lies hid, but nothing is more precious than truth. But you will say, 'How can there be any certain origin to names, when one and the same thing is called by different names, in the several parts of the world?' I answer, of the same thing there may be different causes, of which some people may regard one, and others,

an other. * * * There is therefore no doubt, that of all things, even of words, a reason is to be rendered: and if we know not what that reason is, when we are asked; we ought rather to confess that we do not know, than to affirm that none can be given. I know that Scaliger thinks otherwise; but this is the true account of the matter."

21. "These several observations," he remarks further, "I have unwillingly brought together against those stubborn critics who, while they explode reason from grammar, insist so much on the testimonies of the learned. But have they never read Quintilian, who says, (Lib. i, Cap. 6,) that, 'Language is established by reason, antiquity, authority, and custom?' He therefore does not exclude reason, but makes it the principal thing. Nay, in a manner, Laurentius, and other grammatists, even of their fooleries, are forward to offer *reasons*, such as they are. Moreover, use does not take place without reason; otherwise, it ought to be called abuse, and not use. But from use authority derives all its force; for when it recedes from use, authority becomes nothing: whence Cicero reproves Coelius and Marcus Antonius for speaking according to their own fancy, and not according to use. But, 'Nothing can be lasting,' says Curtius, (Lib. iv,) 'which is not based upon reason.' It remains, therefore, that of all things the reason be first assigned; and then, if it can be done, we may bring forward testimonies; that the thing, having every advantage, may be made the more clear."—*Sanctii Minerva*, Lib. i, Cap. 2.

22. Julius Cæsar Scaliger, from whose opinion Sanctius dissents above, seems to limit the science of grammar to bounds considerably too narrow, though he found within them room for the exercise of much ingenuity and learning. He says, "Grammatica est scientia loquendi ex usu; neque enim constituit regulas scientibus usus modum, sed ex eorum statis frequentibusque usurpatiombus colligit communem rationem loquendi, quam discentibus traderet."—*De Causis L. Latinæ*, Lib. iv, Cap. 76.

"Grammar is the science of speaking according to use; for it does not establish rules for those who know the manner of use, but from the settled and frequent usages of these, gathers the common fashion of speaking, which it should deliver to learners." This limited view seems not only to exclude from the science the use of the pen, but to exempt the learned from any obligation to respect the rules prescribed for the initiation of the young. But I have said, and with abundant authority, that the acquisition of a good style of writing is the main purpose of the study; and, surely, the proficients and adepts in the art can desire for themselves no such exemption. Men of genius, indeed, sometimes affect to despise the pettiness of all grammatical instructions; but this can be nothing else than affectation, since the usage of the learned is confessedly the basis of all such instructions, and several of the loftiest of their own rank appear on the list of grammarians.

23. Quintilian, whose authority is appealed to above, belonged to that age in which the exegesis of histories, poems, and other writings, was considered an essential part of grammar. He therefore, as well as Diomedes, and other ancient writers, divided the grammarian's duties into two parts; the one including what is now called grammar, and the other the explanation of authors, and the stigmatizing of the unworthy. Of the opinion referred to by Sanctius, it seems proper to make here an ampler citation. It shall be attempted in English, though the paragraph is not an easy one to translate. I understand the author to say, "Speakers, too, have their rules to observe; and writers, theirs. Language is established by reason, antiquity, authority, and custom. Of reason the chief ground is analogy, but sometimes etymology. Ancient things have a certain majesty, and, as I might say, religion, to commend them. Authority is wont to be sought from orators and historians; the necessity of metre mostly excuses the poets.

CHAPTER II.

OF GRAMMATICAL AUTHORSHIP.

"Respondeo, dupliciter aliquem dici grammaticum, arte et professione. Grammatici vera arte paucissimi sunt: et hi magna laude digni sunt, ut patuit: hos non vituperant summi viri; quia ipse Plinius ejusmodi grammaticus fuit, et de arte grammatica libelos edidit. Et Grellius veræ grammaticæ fuit diligentissimus doctor; sic et ipse Datus. Alii sunt grammatici professione, et ii plerumque sunt inceptissimi; quia scribimus indocti doctique, et indignissimus quisque hanc sibi artem vindicat:——hos mastigias multis probris docti summo jure insectantur."—DESPAUTER. *Syntaxis*, fol. 1.

1. It is of primary importance in all discussions and expositions of doctrines, of any sort, to ascertain well the *principles* upon which our reasonings are to be founded, and to see that they be such as are immovably established in the nature of things; for error in first principles is fundamental, and he who builds upon an uncertain foundation, incurs at least a *hazard* of seeing his edifice overthrown. The lover of *truth* will be, at all times, diligent to seek it, firm to adhere to it, willing to submit to it, and ready to promote it; but even the truth may be urged unseasonably, and important facts are things liable to be misjoined. It is proper, therefore, for every grammarian gravely to consider, whether and how far the principles

of his philosophy, his politics, his morals, or his religion, ought to influence, or actually do influence, his theory of language, and his practical instructions respecting the right use of words. In practice, grammar is so interwoven with all else that is known, believed, learned, or spoken of among men, that to determine its own peculiar principles with due distinctness, seems to be one of the most difficult points of a grammarian's duty.

2. From misapprehension, narrowness of conception, or improper bias, in relation to this point, many authors have started wrong; denounced others with intemperate zeal; departed themselves from sound doctrine; and produced books which are disgraced not merely by occasional oversights, but by central and radical errors. Hence, too, have sprung up, in the name of grammar, many unprofitable discussions, and whimsical systems of teaching, calculated rather to embarrass than to inform the student. Mere collisions of opinion, conducted without any acknowledged standard to guide the judgement, never tend to real improvement. Grammar is unquestionably a branch of that universal philosophy by which the thoroughly educated mind is enlightened to see all things aright; for philosophy, in this sense of the term, is found in everything. Yet, properly speaking, the true grammarian is not a philosopher, nor can any man strengthen his title to the former character by claiming the latter; and it is certain, that a most disheartening proportion of what in our language has been published under the name of Philosophic Grammar, is equally remote from philosophy, from grammar, and from common sense.

3. True grammar is founded on the authority of reputable custom; and that custom, on the use which men make of their reason. The proofs of what is right are accumulative, and on many points there can be no dispute, because our proofs from the best usage, are both obvious and innumerable. On the other hand, the evidence of what is wrong is rather demonstrative;

for when we would expose a particular error, we exhibit it in contrast with the established principle which it violates. He who formed the erroneous sentence, has in this case no alternative, but either to acknowledge the solecism, or to deny the authority of the rule. There are disputable principles in grammar, as there are moot points in law; but this circumstance affects no settled usage in either; and every person of sense and taste will choose to express himself in the way least liable to censure. All are free indeed from positive constraint on their phraseology; for we do not speak or write by statutes. But the ground of instruction assumed in grammar, is similar to that upon which are established the maxims of *common law,* in jurisprudence. The ultimate principle, then, to which we appeal, as the only true standard of grammatical propriety, is that species of custom which critics denominate GOOD USE; that is, present, reputable, general use.

4. Yet a slight acquaintance with the history of grammar will suffice to show us, that it is much easier to acknowledge this principle, and to commend it in words, than to ascertain what it is, and abide by it in practice. Good use is that which is neither ancient nor recent, neither local nor foreign, neither vulgar nor pedantic; and it will be found that no few have in some way or other departed from it, even while they were pretending to record its dictates. But it is not to be concealed, that in every living language, it is a matter of much inherent difficulty, to reach the standard of propriety, where usage is various; and to ascertain with clearness the decisions of custom, when we descend to minute details. Here is a field in which whatsoever is achieved by the pioneers of literature, can be appreciated only by thorough scholars; for the progress of improvement in any art or science, can be known only to those who can clearly compare its ruder with its more refined stages; and it often happens that what is effected with much labour, may be presented in a very small compass.

5. But the knowledge of grammar may *retrograde*; for whatever loses the vital principle of renovation and growth, tends to decay. And if mere copyists, compilers, abridgers, and modifiers, be encouraged as they now are, it surely will not advance. Style is liable to be antiquated by time, corrupted by innovation, debased by ignorance, perverted by conceit, impaired by negligence, and vitiated by caprice. And nothing but the living spirit of true authorship, and the application of just criticism, can counteract the natural tendency of these causes. English grammar is still in its infancy; and even bears, to the imagination of some, the appearance of a deformed and ugly dwarf among the liberal arts. Treatises are multiplied almost innumerably, but still the old errors survive. Names are rapidly added to our list of authors, while little or nothing is done for the science. Nay, while new blunders have been committed in every new book, old ones have been allowed to stand as by prescriptive right;. and positions that were never true, and sentences that were never good English, have been published and republished under different names, till in our language grammar has become the most ungrammatical of all studies! "Imitators generally copy their originals in an inverse ratio of their merits; that is, by adding as much to their faults, as they lose of their merits."—KNIGHT, *on the Greek Alphabet*, p. 117.

"Who to the life an exact piece would make,
Must not from others' work a copy take."—*Cowley*.

6. All science is laid in the nature of things; and he only who seeks it there, can rightly guide others in the paths of knowledge. He alone can know whether his predecessors went right or wrong, who is capable of a judgement independent of theirs. But with what shameful servility have many false or faulty definitions and rules been copied and copied from one grammar to another, as if authority had canonized their errors, or none had eyes to see them! Whatsoever is dignified and fair, is also modest and

reasonable; but modesty does not consist in having no opinion of one's own, nor reason in following with blind partiality the footsteps of others. Grammar unsupported by authority, is indeed mere fiction. But what apology is this, for that authorship which has produced so many grammars without originality? Shall he who cannot write for himself, improve upon him who can? Shall he who cannot paint, retouch the canvass of Guido? Shall modest ingenuity be allowed only to imitators and to thieves? How many a prefatory argument issues virtually in this! It is not deference to merit, but impudent pretence, practising on the credulity of ignorance! Commonness alone exempts it from scrutiny, and the success it has, is but the wages of its own worthlessness! To read and be informed, is to make a proper use of books for the advancement of learning; but to assume to be an author by editing mere commonplaces and stolen criticisms, is equally beneath the ambition of a scholar and the honesty of a man.

"'T is true, the ancients we may rob with ease;
But who with that mean shift himself can please?"
Sheffield, Duke of Buckingham.

7. Grammar being a practical art, with the principles of which every intelligent person is more or less acquainted, it might be expected that a book written professedly on the subject, should exhibit some evidence of its author's skill. But it would seem that a multitude of bad or indifferent writers have judged themselves qualified to teach the art of speaking and writing well; so that correctness of language and neatness of style are as rarely to be found in grammars as in other books. Nay, I have before suggested that in no other science are the principles of good writing so frequently and so shamefully violated. The code of false grammar embraced in the following work, will go far to sustain this opinion. There have been, however, several excellent scholars, who have thought it an object not unworthy of their talents, to prescribe and elucidate the principles of

English Grammar. But these, with scarcely any exception, have executed their inadequate designs, not as men engaged in their proper calling, but as mere literary almoners, descending for a day from their loftier purposes, to perform a service, needful indeed, and therefore approved, but very far from supplying all the aid that is requisite to a thorough knowledge of the subject. Even the most meritorious have left ample room for improvement, though some have evinced an ability which does honour to themselves, while it gives cause to regret their lack of an inducement to greater labour. The mere grammarian can neither aspire to praise, nor stipulate for a reward; and to those who were best qualified to write, the subject could offer no adequate motive for diligence.

8. Unlearned men, who neither make, nor can make, any pretensions to a knowledge of grammar as a study, if they show themselves modest in what they profess, are by no means to be despised or undervalued for the want of such knowledge. They are subject to no criticism, till they turn authors and write for the public. And even then they are to be treated gently, if they have any thing to communicate, which is worthy to be accepted in a homely dress. Grammatical inaccuracies are to be kindly excused, in all those from whom nothing better can be expected; for people are often under a necessity of appearing as speakers or writers, before they can have learned to write or speak grammatically. The body is more to be regarded than raiment; and the substance of an interesting message, may make the manner of it a little thing. Men of high purposes naturally spurn all that is comparatively low; or all that may seem nice, overwrought, ostentatious, or finical. Hence St. Paul, in writing to the Corinthians, suggests that the design of his preaching might have been defeated, had he affected the orator, and turned his attention to mere "excellency of speech," or "wisdom of words." But this view of things presents no more ground for neglecting grammar, and making coarse and vulgar example our model of speech, than for neglecting dress, and making baize and rags the fashionable costume. The same

apostle exhorts Timothy to "hold fast the form of sound *words*," which he himself had taught him. Nor can it be denied that there is an obligation resting upon all men, to use speech fairly and understandingly. But let it be remembered, that all those upon whose opinions or practices I am disposed to animadvert, are either professed grammarians and philosophers, or authors who, by extraordinary pretensions, have laid themselves under special obligations to be accurate in the use of language. "The *wise in heart* shall be called prudent; and *the sweetness of the lips* increaseth learning."—*Prov.*, xvi, 21. "The words of a man's mouth are as deep waters, and the well-spring of wisdom [is] as a flowing brook."—*Ib.*, xviii, 4. "A fool's mouth is his destruction, and his lips are the snare of his soul."—*Ib.*, xviii, 7.

9. The old maxim recorded by Bacon, "*Loquendum ut vulgus, sentiendum ut sapientes*,"—"We should speak as the vulgar, but think as the wise," is not to be taken without some limitation. For whoever literally speaks as the vulgar, shall offend vastly too much with his tongue, to have either the understanding of the wise or the purity of the good. In all untrained and vulgar minds, the ambition of speaking well is but a dormant or very weak principle. Hence the great mass of uneducated people are lamentably careless of what they utter, both as to the matter and the manner; and no few seem naturally prone to the constant imitation of low example, and some, to the practice of every abuse of which language is susceptible. Hence, as every scholar knows, the least scrupulous of our lexicographers notice many terms but to censure them as "*low*," and omit many more as being beneath their notice. Vulgarity of language, then, ever has been, and ever must be, repudiated by grammarians. Yet we have had pretenders to grammar, who could court the favour of the vulgar, though at the expense of all the daughters of Mnemosyne.

10. Hence the enormous insult to learning and the learned, conveyed in the following scornful quotations: "Grammarians, go to your *tailors* and *shoemakers*, and learn from them the *rational* art of constructing your grammars!"—*Neef's Method of Education*, p. 62. "From a labyrinth without a clew, in which the *most enlightened scholars* of Europe have mazed themselves and misguided others, the author ventures to turn aside."—*Cardell's Gram.*, 12mo, p. 15. Again: "The *nations* of *unlettered men* so adapted their language to philosophic truth, that all physical and intellectual research can find no essential rule to reject or change."—*Ibid.*, p. 91. I have shown that "the nations of unlettered men" are among that portion of the earth's population, upon whose language the genius of grammar has never yet condescended to look down! That people who make no pretensions to learning, can furnish better models or instructions than "the most enlightened scholars," is an opinion which ought not to be disturbed by argument.

11. I regret to say, that even Dr. Webster, with all his obligations and pretensions to literature, has well-nigh taken ground with Neef and Cardell, as above cited; and has not forborne to throw contempt, even on grammar as such, and on men of letters indiscriminately, by supposing the true principles of every language to be best observed and kept by the illiterate. What marvel then, that all his multifarious grammars of the English language are despised? Having suggested that the learned must follow the practice of the populace, because they cannot control it, he adds: "Men of letters may revolt at this suggestion, but if they will attend to the history of our language, they will find the fact to be as here stated. It is commonly supposed that the tendency of this practice of unlettered men is *to corrupt the language*. But the fact is directly the reverse. I am prepared to prove, were it consistent with the nature of this work, that nineteen-twentieths of *all the corruptions* of our language, for five hundred years past, have been introduced by *authors*—men who have made alterations in particular

idioms *which they did not understand*. The same remark is applicable to the *orthography* and *pronunciation*. The tendency of unlettered men is to *uniformity*—to *analogy*; and so strong is this disposition, that the common people have actually converted some of our irregular verbs into regular ones. It is to unlettered people that we owe the disuse of *holpen, bounden, sitten,* and the use of the regular participles, *swelled, helped, worked,* in place of the ancient ones. This popular tendency is not to be contemned and disregarded, as some of the learned affect to do;[3] for it is governed by *the natural, primary principles of all languages,* to which we owe all their regularity and all their melody; viz., a love of uniformity in words of a like character, and a preference of an easy natural pronunciation, and a desire to express the most ideas with the smallest number of words and syllables. It is a fortunate thing for language, that these natural principles generally prevail over arbitrary and artificial rules."—*Webster's Philosophical Gram.*, p. 119; *Improved Gram.*, p. 78. So much for *unlettered erudition!*

12. If every thing that has been taught under the name of grammar, is to be considered as belonging to the science, it will be impossible ever to determine in what estimation the study of it ought to be held; for all that has ever been urged either for or against it, may, upon such a principle, be *proved* by reference to different authorities and irreconcilable opinions. But all who are studious to know, and content to follow, *the fashion* established by the concurrent authority of *the learned*,[4] may at least have some standard to refer to; and if a grammarian's rules be based upon this authority, it must be considered the exclusive privilege of the unlearned to despise them—as it is of the unbred, to contemn the rules of civility. But who shall determine whether the doctrines contained in any given treatise are, or are not, based upon such authority? Who shall decide whether the contributions which any individual may make to our grammatical code, are, or are not, consonant with the best usage? For this, there is no tribunal but the mass of readers, of whom few perhaps are very competent judges. And

here an author's reputation for erudition and judgement, may be available to him: it is the public voice in his favour. Yet every man is at liberty to form his own opinion, and to alter it whenever better knowledge leads him to think differently.

13. But the great misfortune is, that they who need instruction, are not qualified to choose their instructor; and many who must make this choice for their children, have no adequate means of ascertaining either the qualifications of such as offer themselves, or the comparative merits of the different methods by which they profess to teach. Hence this great branch of learning, in itself too comprehensive for the genius or the life of any one man, has ever been open to as various and worthless a set of quacks and plagiaries as have ever figured in any other. There always have been some who knew this, and there may be many who know it now; but the credulity and ignorance which expose so great a majority of mankind to deception and error, are not likely to be soon obviated. With every individual who is so fortunate as to receive any of the benefits of intellectual culture, the whole process of education must begin anew; and, by all that sober minds can credit, the vision of human perfectibility is far enough from any national consummation.

14. Whatever any may think of their own ability, or however some might flout to find their errors censured or their pretensions disallowed; whatever improvement may actually have been made, or however fondly we may listen to boasts and felicitations on that topic; it is presumed, that the general ignorance on the subject of grammar, as above stated, is too obvious to be denied. What then is the remedy? and to whom must our appeal be made? Knowledge cannot be imposed by power, nor is there any domination in the republic of letters. The remedy lies solely in that zeal which can provoke to a generous emulation in the cause of literature; and the appeal, which has recourse to the learning of the learned, and to the

common sense of all, must be pressed home to conviction, till every false doctrine stand refuted, and every weak pretender exposed or neglected. Then shall Science honour them that honour her; and all her triumphs be told, all her instructions be delivered, in "sound speech that cannot be condemned."

15. A generous man is not unwilling to be corrected, and a just one cannot but desire to be set right in all things. Even over noisy gainsayers, a calm and dignified exhibition of true docrine [sic—KTH], has often more influence than ever openly appears. I have even seen the author of a faulty grammar heap upon his corrector more scorn and personal abuse than would fill a large newspaper, and immediately afterwards, in a new edition of his book, renounce the errors which had been pointed out to him, stealing the very language of his amendments from the man whom he had so grossly vilified! It is true that grammarians have ever disputed, and often with more acrimony than discretion. Those who, in elementary treatises, have meddled much with philological controversy, have well illustrated the couplet of Denham: "The tree of knowledge, blasted by disputes, Produces sapless leaves in stead of fruits."

16. Thus, then, as I have before suggested, we find among writers on grammar two numerous classes of authors, who have fallen into opposite errors, perhaps equally reprehensible; the visionaries, and the copyists. The former have ventured upon too much originality, the latter have attempted too little. "The science of philology," says Dr. Alexander Murray, "is not a frivolous study, fit to be conducted by ignorant pedants or visionary enthusiasts. It requires more qualifications to succeed in it, than are usually united in those who pursue it:—a sound penetrating judgement; habits of calm philosophical induction; an erudition various, extensive, and accurate; and a mind likewise, that can direct the knowledge expressed in words, to

illustrate the nature of the signs which convey it."—*Murray's History of European Languages*, Vol. ii, p. 333.

17. They who set aside the authority of custom, and judge every thing to be ungrammatical which appears to them to be unphilosophical, render the whole ground forever disputable, and weary themselves in beating the air. So various have been the notions of this sort of critics, that it would be difficult to mention an opinion not found in some of their books. Amidst this rage for speculation on a subject purely practical, various attempts have been made, to overthrow that system of instruction, which long use has rendered venerable, and long experience proved to be useful. But it is manifestly much easier to raise even plausible objections against this system, than to invent an other less objectionable. Such attempts have generally met the reception they deserved. Their history will give no encouragement to future innovators.

18. Again: While some have thus wasted their energies in eccentric flights, vainly supposing that the learning of ages would give place to their whimsical theories; others, with more success, not better deserved, have multiplied grammars almost innumerably, by abridging or modifying the books they had used in childhood. So that they who are at all acquainted with the origin and character of the various compends thus introduced into our schools, cannot but desire to see them all displaced by some abler and better work, more honourable to its author and more useful to the public, more intelligible to students and more helpful to teachers. Books professedly published for the advancement of knowledge, are very frequently to be reckoned, among its greatest impediments; for the interests of learning are no less injured by whimsical doctrines, than the rights of authorship by plagiarism. Too many of our grammars, profitable only to their makers and venders, are like weights attached to the heels of Hermes. It is discouraging to know the history of this science. But the multiplicity of

treatises already in use, is a reason, not for silence, but for offering more. For, as Lord Bacon observes, the number of ill-written books is not to be diminished by ceasing to write, but by writing others which, like Aaron's serpent, shall swallow up the spurious.[5]

19. I have said that some grammars have too much originality, and others too little. It may be added, that not a few are chargeable with both these faults at once. They are original, or at least anonymous, where there should have been given other authority than that of the compiler's name; and they are copies, or, at best, poor imitations, where the author should have shown himself capable of writing in a good style of his own. What then is the middle ground for the true grammarian? What is the kind, and what the degree, of originality, which are to be commended in works of this sort? In the first place, a grammarian must be a writer, an author, a man who observes and thinks for himself; and not a mere compiler, abridger, modifier, copyist, or plagiarist. Grammar is not the only subject upon which we allow no man to innovate in doctrine; why, then, should it be the only one upon which a man may make it a merit, to work up silently into a book of his own, the best materials found among the instructions of his predecessors and rivals? Some definitions and rules, which in the lapse of time and by frequency of use have become a sort of public property, the grammarian may perhaps be allowed to use at his pleasure; yet even upon these a man of any genius will be apt to set some impress peculiar to himself. But the doctrines of his work ought, in general, to be expressed in his own language, and illustrated by that of others. With respect to quotation, he has all the liberty of other writers, and no more; for, if a grammarian makes "use of his predecessors' labours," why should any one think with Murray, "it is scarcely necessary to apologize for" this, "or for *omitting* to *insert* their names?"—*Introd. to L. Murray's Gram.*, 8vo, p. 7.

20. The author of this volume would here take the liberty briefly to refer to his own procedure. His knowledge of what is *technical* in grammar, was of course chiefly derived from the writings of other grammarians; and to their concurrent opinions and practices, he has always had great respect; yet, in truth, not a line has he ever copied from any of them with a design to save the labour of composition. For, not to compile an English grammar from others already extant, but to compose one more directly from the sources of the art, was the task which he at first proposed to himself. Nor is there in all the present volume a single sentence, not regularly quoted, the authorship of which he supposes may now be ascribed to an other more properly than to himself. Where either authority or acknowledgement was requisite, names have been inserted. In the doctrinal parts of the volume, not only quotations from others, but most examples made for the occasion, are marked with guillemets, to distinguish them from the main text; while, to almost every thing which is really taken from any other known writer, a name or reference is added. For those citations, however, which there was occasion to repeat in different parts of the work, a single reference has sometimes been thought sufficient. This remark refers chiefly to the corrections in the Key, the references being given in the Exercises.

21. Though the theme is not one on which a man may hope to write well with little reflection, it is true that the parts of this treatise which have cost the author the most labour, are those which "consist chiefly of materials selected from the writings of others." These, however, are not the didactical portions of the book, but the proofs and examples; which, according to the custom of the ancient grammarians, ought to be taken from other authors. But so much have the makers of our modern grammars been allowed to presume upon the respect and acquiescence of their readers, that the ancient exactness on this point would often appear pedantic. Many phrases and sentences, either original with the writer, or common to everybody, will therefore be found among the illustrations of the following work; for it was

not supposed that any reader would demand for every thing of this kind the authority of some great name. Anonymous examples are sufficient to elucidate principles, if not to establish them; and elucidation is often the sole purpose for which an example is needed.

22. It is obvious enough, that no writer on grammar has any right to propose himself as authority for what he teaches; for every language, being the common property of all who use it, ought to be carefully guarded against the caprices of individuals; and especially against that presumption which might attempt to impose erroneous or arbitrary definitions and rules. "Since the matter of which we are treating," says the philologist of Salamanca, "is to be verified, first by reason, and then by testimony and usage, none ought to wonder if we sometimes deviate from the track of great men; for, with whatever authority any grammarian may weigh with me, unless he shall have confirmed his assertions by reason, and also by examples, he shall win no confidence in respect to grammar. For, as Seneca says, Epistle 95, 'Grammarians are the *guardians*, not the *authors*, of language.'"—*Sanctii Minerva*, Lib. ii, Cap. 2. Yet, as what is intuitively seen to be true or false, is already sufficiently proved or detected, many points in grammar need nothing more than to be clearly stated and illustrated; nay, it would seem an injurious reflection on the understanding of the reader, to accumulate proofs of what cannot but be evident to all who speak the language.

23. Among men of the same profession, there is an unavoidable rivalry, so far as they become competitors for the same prize; but in competition there is nothing dishonourable, while excellence alone obtains distinction, and no advantage is sought by unfair means. It is evident that we ought to account him the best grammarian, who has the most completely executed the worthiest design. But no worthy design can need a false apology; and it is worse than idle to prevaricate. That is but a spurious modesty, which

prompts a man to disclaim in one way what he assumes in an other—or to underrate the duties of his office, that he may boast of having "done all that could reasonably be expected." Whoever professes to have improved the science of English grammar, must claim to know more of the matter than the generality of English grammarians; and he who begins with saying, that "little can be expected" from the office he assumes, must be wrongfully contradicted, when he is held to have done much. Neither the ordinary power of speech, nor even the ability to write respectably on common topics, makes a man a critic among critics, or enables him to judge of literary merit. And if, by virtue of these qualifications alone, a man will become a grammarian or a connoisseur, he can hold the rank only by courtesy—a courtesy which is content to degrade the character, that his inferior pretensions may be accepted and honoured under the name.

24. By the force of a late popular example, still too widely influential, grammatical authorship has been reduced, in the view of many, to little or nothing more than a mere serving-up of materials anonymously borrowed; and, what is most remarkable, even for an indifferent performance of this low office, not only unnamed reviewers, but several writers of note, have not scrupled to bestow the highest praise of grammatical excellence! And thus the palm of superior skill in grammar, has been borne away by a *professed compiler*; who had so mean an opinion of what his theme required, as to deny it even the common courtesies of compilation! What marvel is it, that, under the wing of such authority, many writers have since sprung up, to improve upon this most happy design; while all who were competent to the task, have been discouraged from attempting any thing like a complete grammar of our language? What motive shall excite a man to long-continued diligence, where such notions prevail as give mastership no hope of preference, and where the praise of his ingenuity and the reward of his labour must needs be inconsiderable, till some honoured compiler usurp them both, and bring his "most useful matter" before the world under

better auspices? If the love of learning supply such a motive, who that has generously yielded to the impulse, will not now, like Johnson, feel himself reduced to an "humble drudge"—or, like Perizonius, apologize for the apparent folly of devoting his time to such a subject as grammar?

25. The first edition of the "Institutes of English Grammar," the doctrinal parts of which are embraced in the present more copious work, was published in the year 1823; since which time, (within the space of twelve years,) about forty new compends, mostly professing to be abstracts of *Murray*, with improvements, have been added to our list of English grammars. The author has examined as many as thirty of them, and seen advertisements of perhaps a dozen more. Being various in character, they will of course be variously estimated; but, so far as he can judge, they are, without exception, works of little or no real merit, and not likely to be much patronized or long preserved from oblivion. For which reason, he would have been inclined entirely to disregard the petty depredations which the writers of several of them have committed upon his earlier text, were it not possible, that by such a frittering-away of his work, he himself might one day seem to some to have copied that from others which was first taken from him. Trusting to make it manifest to men of learning, that in the production of the books which bear his name, far more has been done for the grammar of our language than any single hand had before achieved within the scope of practical philology, and that with perfect fairness towards other writers; he cannot but feel a wish that the integrity of his text should be preserved, whatever else may befall; and that the multitude of scribblers who judge it so needful to remodel Murray's defective compilation, would forbear to publish under his name or their own what they find only in the following pages.

26. The mere rivalry of their authorship is no subject of concern; but it is enough for any ingenuous man to have toiled for years in solitude to

complete a work of public utility, without entering a warfare for life to defend and preserve it. Accidental coincidences in books are unfrequent, and not often such as to excite the suspicion of the most sensitive. But, though the criteria of plagiarism are neither obscure nor disputable, it is not easy, in this beaten track of literature, for persons of little reading to know what is, or is not, original. Dates must be accurately observed; and a multitude of minute things must be minutely compared. And who will undertake such a task but he that is personally interested? Of the thousands who are forced into the paths of learning, few ever care to know, by what pioneer, or with what labour, their way was cast up for them. And even of those who are honestly engaged in teaching, not many are adequate judges of the comparative merits of the great number of books on this subject. The common notions of mankind conform more easily to fashion than to truth; and even of some things within their reach, the majority seem contend to take their opinions upon trust. Hence, it is vain to expect that that which is intrinsically best, will be everywhere preferred; or that which is meritoriously elaborate, adequately appreciated. But common sense might dictate, that learning is not encouraged or respected by those who, for the making of books, prefer a pair of scissors to the pen.

27. The fortune of a grammar is not always an accurate test of its merits. The goddess of the plenteous horn stands blindfold yet upon the floating prow; and, under her capricious favour, any pirate-craft, ill stowed with plunder, may sometimes speed as well, as barges richly laden from the golden mines of science. Far more are now afloat, and more are stranded on dry shelves, than can be here reported. But what this work contains, is candidly designed to qualify the reader to be himself a judge of what it *should* contain; and I will hope, so ample a report as this, being thought sufficient, will also meet his approbation. The favour of one discerning mind that comprehends my subject, is worth intrinsically more than that of

half the nation: I mean, of course, the half of whom my gentle reader is not one.

"They praise and they admire they know not what,
And know not whom, but as one leads the other."—*Milton*.

CHAPTER III.

OF GRAMMATICAL SUCCESS AND FAME.

"Non is ego sum, cui aut jucundum, aut adeo opus sit, de aliis detrahere, et hac viâ ad famara contendere. Melioribus artibus laudem parare didici. Itaque non libenter dico, quod præsens institutum dicere cogit."—Jo. AUGUSTI ERNESTI *Præf. ad Græcum Lexicon*, p. vii.

1. The real history of grammar is little known; and many erroneous impressions are entertained concerning it: because the story of the systems most generally received has never been fully told; and that of a multitude now gone to oblivion was never worth telling. In the distribution of grammatical fame, which has chiefly been made by the hand of interest, we have had a strange illustration of the saying: "Unto every one that hath shall be given, and he shall have abundance; but from him that hath not, shall be taken away even that which he hath." Some whom fortune has made popular, have been greatly overrated, if learning and talent are to be taken into the account; since it is manifest, that with no extraordinary claims to either, they have taken the very foremost rank among grammarians, and thrown the learning and talents of others into the shade, or made them tributary to their own success and popularity.

2. It is an ungrateful task to correct public opinion by showing the injustice of praise. Fame, though it may have been both unexpected and undeserved, is apt to be claimed and valued as part and parcel of a man's good name; and the dissenting critic, though ever-so candid, is liable to be thought an envious detractor. It would seem in general most prudent to leave mankind to find out for themselves how far any commendation bestowed on individuals is inconsistent with truth. But, be it remembered, that celebrity is not a virtue; nor, on the other hand, is experience the cheapest of teachers. A good man may not have done all things ably and well; and it is certainly no small mistake to estimate his character by the current value of his copy-rights. Criticism may destroy the reputation of a book, and not be inconsistent with a cordial respect for the private worth of its author. The reader will not be likely to be displeased with what is to be stated in this chapter, if he can believe, that no man's merit as a writer, may well be enhanced by ascribing to him that which he himself, for the protection of his own honour, has been constrained to disclaim. He cannot suppose that too much is alleged, if he will admit that a grammarian's fame should be thought safe enough in his *own keeping.* Are authors apt to undervalue their own performances? Or because proprietors and publishers may profit by the credit of a book, shall it be thought illiberal to criticise it? Is the author himself to be disbelieved, that the extravagant praises bestowed upon him may be justified? "Superlative commendation," says Dillwyn, "is near akin to *detraction.*" (See his *Reflections,* p. 22.) Let him, therefore, who will charge detraction upon me, first understand wherein it consists. I shall criticise, freely, both the works of the living, and the doctrines of those who, to us, live only in their works; and if any man dislike this freedom, let him rebuke it, showing wherein it is wrong or unfair. The amiable author just quoted, says again: "Praise has so often proved an *impostor,* that it would be well, wherever we meet with it, to treat

it as a vagrant."—*Ib.*, p. 100. I go not so far as this; but that eulogy which one knows to be false, he cannot but reckon impertinent.

3. Few writers on grammar have been more noted than WILLIAM LILY and LINDLEY MURRAY. Others have left better monuments of their learning and talents, but none perhaps have had greater success and fame. The Latin grammar which was for a long time most popular in England, has commonly been ascribed to the one; and what the Imperial Review, in 1805, pronounced "the best English grammar, beyond all comparison, that has yet appeared," was compiled by the other. And doubtless they have both been rightly judged to excel the generality of those which they were intended to supersede; and both, in their day, may have been highly serviceable to the cause of learning. For all excellence is but comparative; and to grant them this superiority, is neither to prefer them now, nor to justify the praise which has been bestowed upon their authorship. As the science of grammar can never be taught without a book, or properly taught by any book which is not itself grammatical, it is of some importance both to teachers and to students, to make choice of the best. Knowledge will not advance where grammars hold rank by prescription. Yet it is possible that many, in learning to write and speak, may have derived no inconsiderable benefit from a book that is neither accurate nor complete.

4. With respect to time, these two grammarians were three centuries apart; during which period, the English language received its most classical refinement, and the relative estimation of the two studies, Latin and English grammar, became in a great measure reversed. Lily was an Englishman, born at Odiham,[6] in Hampshire, in 1466. When he had arrived at manhood, he went on a pilgrimage to Jerusalem; and while abroad studied some time at Rome, and also at Paris. On his return he was thought one of the most accomplished scholars in England. In 1510, Dr. John Colet, dean of St. Paul's church, in London, appointed him the first high master of St.

Paul's School, then recently founded by this gentleman's munificence. In this situation, Lily appears to have taught with great credit to himself till 1522, when he died of the plague, at the age of 56. For the use of this school, he wrote and published certain parts of the grammar which has since borne his name. Of the authorship of this work many curious particulars are stated in the preface by John Ward, which may be seen in the edition of 1793. Lily had able rivals, as well as learned coadjutors and friends. By the aid of the latter, he took precedence of the former; and his publications, though not voluminous, soon gained a general popularity. So that when an arbitrary king saw fit to silence competition among the philologists, by becoming himself, as Sir Thomas Elliott says, "the chiefe authour and setter-forth of an introduction into grammar, for the childrene of his lovynge subjects," Lily's Grammar was preferred for the basis of the standard. Hence, after the publishing of it became a privilege patented by the crown, the book appears to have been honoured with a royal title, and to have been familiarly called King Henry's Grammar.

5. Prefixed to this book, there appears a very ancient epistle to the reader, which while it shows the reasons for this royal interference with grammar, shows also, what is worthy of remembrance, that guarded and maintained as it was, even royal interference was here ineffectual to its purpose. It neither produced uniformity in the methods of teaching, nor, even for instruction in a dead language, entirely prevented the old manual from becoming diverse in its different editions. The style also may serve to illustrate what I have elsewhere said about the duties of a modern grammarian. "As for the diversitie of grammars, it is well and profitably taken awaie by the King's Majesties wisdome; who, foreseeing the inconvenience, and favorably providing the remedie, caused one kind of grammar by sundry learned men to be diligently drawn, and so to be set out, only every where to be taught, for the use of learners, and for the hurt in changing of schoolemaisters." That is, to prevent the injury which schoolmasters were doing by a

whimsical choice, or frequent changing, of grammars. But, says the letter, "The varietie of teaching is divers yet, and alwaies will be; for that every schoolemaister liketh that he knoweth, and seeth not the use of that he knoweth not; and therefore judgeth that the most sufficient waie, which he seeth to be the readiest meane, and perfectest kinde, to bring a learner to have a thorough knowledge therein." The only remedy for such an evil then is, to teach those who are to be teachers, and to desert all who, for any whim of their own, desert sound doctrine.

6. But, to return. A law was made in England by Henry the Eighth, commanding Lily's Grammar only, (or that which has commonly been quoted as Lily's,) to be everywhere adopted and taught, as the common standard of grammatical instruction.[7] Being long kept in force by means of a special inquiry, directed to be made by the bishops at their stated visitations, this law, for three hundred years, imposed the book on all the established schools of the realm. Yet it is certain, that about one half of what has thus gone under the name of Lily, ("because," says one of the patentees, "he had *so considerable a hand* in the composition,") was written by Dr. Colet, by Erasmus, or by others who improved the work after Lily's death. And of the other half, it has been incidentally asserted in history, that neither the scheme nor the text was original. The Printer's Grammar, London, 1787, speaking of the art of type-foundery, says: "The Italians in a short time brought it to *that* perfection, that in the beginning of the year 1474, they cast a letter not much inferior to the best types of the present age; as may be seen in a Latin Grammar, written by Omnibonus Leonicenus, and printed at Padua on the 14th of January, 1474; *from whom our grammarian, Lily, has taken the entire scheme of his Grammar, and transcribed the greatest part thereof, without paying any regard to the memory of this author.*" The historian then proceeds to speak about types. See also the same thing in the History of Printing, 8vo, London, 1770. This

is the grammar which bears upon its title page: "*Quam solam Regia Majestas in omnibus scholis docendam prcæcipit.*"

7. Murray was an intelligent and very worthy man, to whose various labours in the compilation of books our schools are under many obligations. But in original thought and critical skill he fell far below most of "the authors to whom," he confesses, "the grammatical part of his compilation is *principally indebted for its materials*; namely, Harris, Johnson, Lowth, Priestley, Beattie, Sheridan, Walker, Coote, Blair, and Campbell."—*Introd. to Lindley Murray's Gram.*, p. 7. It is certain and evident that he entered upon his task with a very insufficient preparation. His biography, which was commenced by himself and completed by one of his most partial friends, informs us, that, "Grammar did not particularly engage his attention, until a short time previous to the publication of his first work on that subject;" that, "His Grammar, as it appeared in the first edition, was completed in rather less than a year;" that, "It was begun in the spring of 1794, and published in the spring of 1795—though he had an intervening illness, which, for several weeks, stopped the progress of the work;" and that, "The Exercises and Key were also composed in about a year."—*Life of L. Murray*, p. 188. From the very first sentence of his book, it appears that he entertained but a low and most erroneous idea of the duties of that sort of character in which he was about to come before the public.[8] He improperly imagined, as many others have done, that "little can be expected" from a modern grammarian, or (as he chose to express it) "from a *new compilation*, besides a careful selection of the most useful matter, and some degree of improvement in the mode of adapting it to the understanding, and the gradual progress of learners."—*Introd. to L. Murray's Gram.*; 8vo, p. 5; 12mo, p. 3. As if, to be master of his own art—to think and write well himself, were no part of a grammarian's business! And again, as if the jewels of scholarship, thus carefully selected, could need a burnish or a foil from other hands than those which fashioned them!

8. Murray's general idea of the doctrines of grammar was judicious. He attempted no broad innovation on what had been previously taught; for he had neither the vanity to suppose he could give currency to novelties, nor the folly to waste his time in labours utterly nugatory. By turning his own abilities to their best account, he seems to have done much to promote and facilitate the study of our language. But his notion of grammatical authorship, cuts off from it all pretence to literary merit, for the sake of doing good; and, taken in any other sense than as a forced apology for his own assumptions, his language on this point is highly injurious towards the very authors whom he copied. To justify himself, he ungenerously places them, in common with others, under a degrading necessity which no able grammarian ever felt, and which every man of genius or learning must repudiate. If none of our older grammars disprove his assertion, it is time to have a new one that will; for, to expect the perfection of grammar from him who cannot treat the subject in a style at once original and pure, is absurd. He says, "The greater part of an English grammar *must necessarily be a compilation* ;" and adds, with reference to his own, "originality belongs to but a small portion of it. This I have acknowledged; and I trust *this acknowledgement* will protect me from all attacks, grounded on any supposed unjust and irregular assumptions." This quotation is from a letter addressed by Murray to his American publishers, in 1811, after they had informed him of certain complaints respecting the liberties which he had taken in his work. See "*The Friend*," Vol. iii, p. 34.

9. The acknowledgement on which he thus relies, does not appear to have been made, till his grammar had gone through several editions. It was, however, at some period, introduced into his short preface, or "Introduction," in the following well-meant but singularly sophistical terms: "In *a work* which professes itself to be a *compilation*, and which, *from the nature and design of it*, must consist chiefly of materials selected from the writings of others, *it is scarcely necessary to apologise* for the use which

the Compiler has made of his predecessors' labours, or for *omitting to insert their names. From the alterations* which have been frequently made in the sentiments and the language, to suit the connexion, and to adapt them to the particular purposes for which they are introduced; and, in many instances, *from the uncertainty to whom* the passages originally belonged, the insertion of names *could seldom be made with propriety*. But if this could have been generally done, a work of this nature *would derive no advantage from it*, equal to the inconvenience of crowding the pages with a repetition of names and references. It is. however, proper to acknowledge, in general terms, that the authors to whom the grammatical part of this compilation is principally indebted for its materials, are Harris, Johnson, Lowth, Priestley, Beattie, Sheridan, Walker, and Coote."—*Introd.; Duodecimo Gram.*, p. 4; *Octavo*, p. 7.

10. The fallacy, or absurdity, of this language sprung from necessity. An impossible case was to be made out. For compilation, though ever so fair, is not grammatical authorship. But some of the commenders of Murray have not only professed themselves satisfied with this general acknowledgement, but have found in it a candour and a liberality, a modesty and a diffidence, which, as they allege, ought to protect him from all animadversion. Are they friends to learning? Let them calmly consider what I reluctantly offer for its defence and promotion. In one of the recommendations appended to Murray's grammars, it *is* said, "They have nearly superseded every thing else of the kind, by concentrating the remarks of the best authors on the subject." But, in truth, with several of the best English grammars published previously to his own, Murray appears to have been totally unacquainted. The chief, if not the only school grammars which were largely copied by him, were Lowth's and Priestley's, though others perhaps may have shared the fate of these in being "superseded" by his. It may be seen by inspection, that in copying these two authors, the compiler, agreeably to what he says above, omitted all names and references—even such as they had

scrupulously inserted: and, at the outset, assumed to be himself the sole authority for all his doctrines and illustrations; satisfying his own mind with making, some years afterwards, that general apology which we are now criticising. For if he so mutilated and altered the passages which he adopted, as to make it improper to add the names of their authors, upon what other authority than his own do they rest? But if, on the other hand, he generally copied without alteration; his examples are still anonymous, while his first reason for leaving them so, is plainly destroyed: because his position is thus far contradicted by the fact.

11. In his later editions, however, there are two opinions which the compiler thought proper to support by regular quotations; and, now and then, in other instances, the name of an author appears. The two positions thus distinguished, are these: *First*, That the noun *means* is necessarily singular as well as plural, so that one cannot with propriety use the singular form, *mean*, to signify that by which an end is attained; *Second*, That the subjective mood, to which he himself had previously given all the tenses without inflection, is not different in form from the indicative, except in the present tense. With regard to the later point, I have shown, in its proper place, that he taught erroneously, both before and after he changed his opinion; and concerning the former, the most that can be proved by quotation, is, that both *mean* and *means* for the singular number, long have been, and still are, in good use, or sanctioned by many elegant writers; so that either form may yet be considered grammatical, though the irregular can claim to be so, only when it is used in this particular sense. As to his second reason for the suppression of names, to wit, "the *uncertainty to whom* the passages originally belonged,"—to make the most of it, it is but partial and relative; and, surely, no other grammar ever before so multiplied the difficulty in the eyes of teachers, and so widened the field for commonplace authorship, as has the compilation in question. The origin of a sentiment or passage may be uncertain to one man, and perfectly well

known to an other. The embarrassment which a *compiler* may happen to find from this source, is worthy of little sympathy. For he cannot but know from what work he is taking any particular sentence or paragraph, and those parts of a *grammar,* which are new to the eye of a great grammarian, may very well be credited to him who claims to have written the book. I have thus disposed of his second reason for the omission of names and references, in compilations of grammar.

12. There remains one more: "A work of this nature *would derive no advantage from it,* equal to the inconvenience of crowding the pages with a repetition of names and references." With regard to a small work, in which the matter is to be very closely condensed, this argument has considerable force. But Murray has in general allowed himself very ample room, especially in his two octavoes. In these, and for the most part also in his duodecimoes, all needful references might easily have been added without increasing the size of his volumes, or injuring their appearance. In nine cases out of ten, the names would only have been occupied what is now blank space. It is to be remembered, that these books do not differ much, except in quantity of paper. His octavo Grammar is but little more than a reprint, in a larger type, of the duodecimo Grammar, together with his Exercises and Key. The demand for this expensive publication has been comparatively small; and it is chiefly to the others, that the author owes his popularity as a grammarian. As to the advantage which Murray or his work might have derived from an adherence on his part to the usual custom of compilers, *that* may be variously estimated. The remarks of the best grammarians or the sentiments of the best authors, are hardly to be thought the more worthy of acceptance, for being concentrated in such a manner as to merge their authenticity in the fame of the copyist. Let me not be understood to suggest that this good man sought popularity at the expense of others; for I do not believe that either fame or interest was his motive. But the right of authors to the credit of their writings, is a delicate point;

and, surely, his example would have been worthier of imitation, had he left no ground for the foregoing objections, and carefully barred the way to any such interference.

13. But let the first sentence of this apology be now considered. It is here suggested, that because this work is a compilation, even such an acknowledgement as the author makes, is "scarcely necessary." This is too much to say. Yet one may readily admit, that a compilation, "from the nature and design of it, must consist chiefly"—nay, *wholly*—"of materials selected from the writings of others." But what able grammarian would ever willingly throw himself upon the horns of such a dilemma! The nature and design *of a book,* whatever they may be, are matters for which the author alone is answerable; but the nature and design *of grammar,* are no less repugnant to the strain of this apology, than to the vast number of errors and defects which were overlooked by Murray in his work of compilation. It is the express purpose of this practical science, to enable a man to write well himself. He that cannot do this, exhibits no excess of modesty when he claims to have "done all that could reasonably be expected in a work of this nature."—*L. Murray's Gram., Introd.,* p. 9. He that sees with other men's eyes, is peculiarly liable to errors and inconsistencies: uniformity is seldom found in patchwork, or accuracy in secondhand literature. Correctness of language is in the mind, rather than in the hand or the tongue; and, in order to secure it, some originality of thought is necessary. A delineation from new surveys is not the less original because the same region has been sketched before; and how can he be the ablest of surveyors, who, through lack of skill or industry, does little more than transcribe the field-notes and copy the projections of his predecessors?

14. This author's oversights are numerous. There is no part of the volume more accurate than that which he literally copied from Lowth. To the Short Introduction alone, he was indebted for more than a hundred and twenty

paragraphs; and even in these there are many things obviously erroneous. Many of the best practical notes were taken from Priestley; yet it was he, at whose doctrines were pointed most of those "positions and discussions," which alone the author claims as original. To some of these reasonings, however, his own alterations may have given rise; for, where he "persuades himself he is not destitute of originality," he is often arguing against the text of his own earlier editions. Webster's well-known complaints of Murray's unfairness, had a far better cause than requital; for there was no generosity in ascribing them to peevishness, though the passages in question were not worth copying. On perspicuity and accuracy, about sixty pages were extracted from Blair; and it requires no great critical acumen to discover, that they are miserably deficient in both. On the law of language, there are fifteen pages from Campbell; which, with a few exceptions, are well written. The rules for spelling are the same as Walker's: the third one, however, is a gross blunder; and the fourth, a, needless repetition.

15. Were this a place for minute criticism, blemishes almost innumerable might be pointed out. It might easily be shown that almost every rule laid down in the book for the observance of the learner, was repeatedly violated by the hand of the master. Nor is there among all those who have since abridged or modified the work, an abler grammarian than he who compiled it. Who will pretend that Flint, Alden, Comly, Jaudon, Russell, Bacon, Lyon, Miller, Alger, Maltby, Ingersoll, Fisk, Greenleaf, Merchant, Kirkham, Cooper, R. G. Greene, Woodworth, Smith, or Frost, has exhibited greater skill? It is curious to observe, how frequently a grammatical blunder committed by Murray, or some one of his predecessors, has escaped the notice of all these, as well as of many others who have found it easier to copy him than to write for themselves. No man professing to have copied and improved Murray, can rationally be supposed to have greatly excelled him; for to pretend to have produced an *improved copy of a compilation*, is to claim a sort of authorship, even inferior to his, and utterly unworthy of

any man who is able to prescribe and elucidate the principles of English grammar.

16. But Murray's grammatical works, being extolled in the reviews, and made common stock in trade,—being published, both in England and in America, by booksellers of the most extensive correspondence, and highly commended even by those who were most interested in the sale of them,—have been eminently successful with the public; and in the opinion of the world, success is the strongest proof of merit. Nor has the force of this argument been overlooked by those who have written in aid of his popularity. It is the strong point in most of the commendations which have been bestowed upon Murray as a grammarian. A recent eulogist computes, that, "at least five millions of copies of his various school-books have been printed;" particularly commends him for his "candour and liberality towards rival authors;" avers that, "he went on, examining and correcting his Grammar, through all its forty editions, till he brought it to a degree of perfection which will render it as permanent as the English language itself;" censures (and not without reason) the "presumption" of those "superficial critics" who have attempted to amend the work, and usurp his honours; and, regarding the compiler's confession of his indebtedness to others, but as a mark of "his exemplary diffidence of his own merits," adds, (in very bad English,) "Perhaps there never was an author whose success and fame were more *unexpected by himself than Lindley Murray.*"—The Friend, Vol. iii, p. 33.

17. In a New-York edition of Murray's Grammar, printed in 1812, there was inserted a "Caution to the Public," by Collins & Co., his American correspondents and publishers, in which are set forth the unparalleled success and merit of the work, "as it came *in purity* from the pen of the author;" with an earnest remonstrance against the several *revised editions* which had appeared at Boston, Philadelphia, and other places, and against

the unwarrantable liberties taken by American teachers, in altering the work, under pretence of improving it. In this article it is stated, "that *the whole* of these mutilated editions *have been seen* and examined by Lindley Murray himself, and that they, have met with *his decided disapprobation.* Every rational mind," continue these gentlemen, "will agree with him, that, 'the *rights of living authors,* and the *interests of science and literature,* demand the abolition of this *ungenerous practice.*'" (See this also in *Murray's Key,* 12mo, N. Y., 1811, p. iii.) Here, then, we have the feeling and opinion of Murray himself, upon this tender point of right. Here we see the tables turned, and other men judging it "scarcely necessary to apologize for the use which *they have made* of their predecessors' labours."

18. It is really remarkable to find an author and his admirers so much at variance, as are Murray and his commenders, in relation to his grammatical authorship; and yet, under what circumstances could men have stronger desires to avoid apparent contradiction? They, on the one side, claim for him the highest degree of merit as a grammarian; and continue to applaud his works as if nothing more could be desired in the study of English grammar—a branch of learning which some of them are willing emphatically to call "*his* science." He, on the contrary, to avert the charge of plagiarism, disclaims almost every thing in which any degree of literary merit consists; supposes it impossible to write an English grammar the greater part of which is not a "compilation;" acknowledges that originality belongs to but a small part of his own; trusts that such a general acknowledgement will protect him from all censure; suppresses the names of other writers, and leaves his examples to rest solely on his own authority; and, "contented with the great respectability of his private character and station, is satisfied with being *useful* as an author."—*The Friend,* Vol. iii, p. 33. By the high praises bestowed upon his works, his own voice is overborne: the trumpet of fame has drowned it. His liberal authorship is profitable in trade, and interest has power to swell and prolong the strain.

19. The name and character of Lindley Murray are too venerable to allow us to approach even the errors of his grammars, without some recognition of the respect due to his personal virtues and benevolent intentions. For the private virtues of Murray, I entertain as cordial a respect as any other man. Nothing is argued against these, even if it be proved that causes independent of true literary merit have given him his great and unexpected fame as a grammarian. It is not intended by the introduction of these notices, to impute to him any thing more or less than what his own words plainly imply; except those inaccuracies and deficiencies which still disgrace his work as a literary performance, and which of course he did not discover. He himself knew that he had not brought the book to such perfection as has been ascribed to it; for, by way of apology for his frequent alterations, he says, "Works of this nature admit of repeated improvements; and are, perhaps, never complete." Necessity has urged this reasoning upon me. I am as far from any invidious feeling, or any sordid motive, as was Lindley Murray. But it is due to truth, to correct erroneous impressions; and, in order to obtain from some an impartial examination of the following pages, it seemed necessary first to convince them, *that it is possible* to compose a better grammar than Murray's, without being particularly indebted to him. If this treatise is not such, a great deal of time has been thrown away upon a useless project; and if it is, the achievement is no fit subject for either pride or envy. It differs from his, and from all the pretended amendments of his, as a new map, drawn from actual and minute surveys, differs from an old one, compiled chiefly from others still older and confessedly still more imperfect. The region and the scope are essentially the same; the tracing and the colouring are more original; and (if the reader can pardon the suggestion) perhaps more accurate and vivid.

20. He who makes a new grammar, does nothing for the advancement of learning, unless his performance excel all earlier ones designed for the same purpose; and nothing for his own honour, unless such excellence result from

the exercise of his own ingenuity and taste. A good style naturally commends itself to every reader—even to him who cannot tell why it is worthy of preference. Hence there is reason to believe, that the true principles of practical grammar, deduced from custom and sanctioned by time, will never be generally superseded by any thing which individual caprice may substitute. In the republic of letters, there will always be some who can distinguish merit; and it is impossible that these should ever be converted to any whimsical theory of language, which goes to make void the learning of past ages. There will always be some who can discern the difference between originality of style, and innovation in doctrine,—between a due regard to the opinions of others, and an actual usurpation of their text; and it is incredible that these should ever be satisfied with any mere compilation of grammar, or with any such authorship as either confesses or betrays the writer's own incompetence. For it is not true, that, "an English grammar must necessarily be," in any considerable degree, if at all, "a compilation;" nay, on such a theme, and in "the grammatical part" of the work, all compilation beyond a fair use of authorities regularly quoted, or of materials either voluntarily furnished or free to all, most unavoidably implies—not conscious "ability," generously doing honour to rival merit—nor "exemplary diffidence," modestly veiling its own—but inadequate skill and inferior talents, bribing the public by the spoils of genius, and seeking precedence by such means as not even the purest desire of doing good can justify.

21. Among the professed copiers of Murray, there is not one to whom the foregoing remarks do not apply, as forcibly as to him. For no one of them all has attempted any thing more honourable to himself, or more beneficial to the public, than what their master had before achieved; nor is there any one, who, with the same disinterestedness, has guarded his design from the imputation of a pecuniary motive. It is comical to observe what they say in their prefaces. Between praise to sustain their choice of a model, and blame

to make room for their pretended amendments, they are often placed in as awkward a dilemma, as that which was contrived when grammar was identified with compilation. I should have much to say, were I to show them all in their true light.[9] Few of them have had such success as to be worthy of notice here; but the names of many will find frequent place in my code of false grammar. The one who seems to be now taking the lead in fame and revenue, filled with glad wonder at his own popularity, is SAMUEL KIRKHAM. Upon this gentleman's performance, I shall therefore bestow a few brief observations. If I do not overrate this author's literary importance, a fair exhibition of the character of his grammar, may be made an instructive lesson to some of our modern literati. The book is a striking sample of a numerous species.

22. Kirkham's treatise is entitled, "English Grammar *in familiar Lectures*, accompanied by a *Compendium*;" that is, by a folded sheet. Of this work, of which I have recently seen copies purporting to be of the "SIXTY-SEVENTH EDITION," and others again of the "HUNDRED AND FIFTH EDITION," each published at Baltimore in 1835, I can give no earlier account, than what may be derived from the "SECOND EDITION, enlarged and much improved," which was published at Harrisburg in 1825. The preface, which appears to have been written for his *first* edition, is dated, "Fredericktown, Md., August 22, 1823." In it, there is no recognition of any obligation to Murray, or to any other grammarian in particular; but with the modest assumption, that the style of the "best philologists," needed to be retouched, the book is presented to the world under the following pretensions:

"The author of this production has endeavoured to condense *all the most important subject-matter of the whole science,* and present it in so small a compass that the learner can become familiarly acquainted with it in a *short time.* He makes but small pretensions to originality in theoretical matter.

Most of the principles laid down, have been selected from our *best modern philologists*. If his work is entitled to any degree of *merit*, it is not on account of a judicious selection of principles and rules, but for the easy mode adopted of communicating *these* to the mind of the learner."—*Kirkham's Grammar*, 1825, p. 10.

23. It will be found on examination, that what this author regarded as *"all the most important subject-matter of the whole science"* of grammar, included nothing more than the most common elements of the orthography, etymology, and syntax, of the English tongue—beyond which his scholarship appears not to have extended. Whatsoever relates to derivation, to the sounds of the letters, to prosody, (as punctuation, utterance, figures, versification, and poetic diction,) found no place in his "comprehensive system of grammar;" nor do his later editions treat any of these things amply or well. In short, he treats nothing well; for he is a bad writer. Commencing his career of authorship under circumstances the most forbidding, yet receiving encouragement from commendations bestowed in pity, he proceeded, like a man of business, to profit mainly by the chance; and, without ever acquiring either the feelings or the habits of a scholar, soon learned by experience that, "It is much better to *write* than [to] *starve*."—*Kirkham's Gram., Stereotyped*, p. 89. It is cruel in any man, to look narrowly into the faults of an author who peddles a school-book for bread. The starveling wretch whose defence and plea are poverty and sickness, demands, and must have, in the name of humanity, an immunity from criticism, if not the patronage of the public. Far be it from me, to notice any such character, except with kindness and charity. Nor need I be told, that tenderness is due to the "young;" or that noble results sometimes follow unhopeful beginnings. These things are understood and duly appreciated. The gentleman was young once, even as he says; and I, his equal in years, was then, in authorship, as young—though, it were to be hoped, not quite so immature. But, as circumstances alter cases, so time and

chance alter circumstances. Under no circumstances, however, can the artifices of quackery be thought excusable in him who claims to be the very greatest of modern grammarians. The niche that in the temple of learning belongs to any individual, can be no other than that which his own labours have purchased: here, his *own merit* alone must be his pedestal. If this critical sketch be unimpeachably *just*, its publication requires no further warrant. The correction has been forborne, till the subject of it has become rich, and popular, and proud; proud enough at least to have published his utter contempt for me and all my works. Yet not for this do I judge him worthy of notice here, but merely as an apt example of some men's grammatical success and fame. The ways and means to these grand results are what I purpose now to consider.

24. The common supposition, that the world is steadily advancing in knowledge and improvement, would seem to imply, that the man who could plausibly boast of being the most successful and most popular grammarian of the nineteenth century, cannot but be a scholar of such merit as to deserve some place, if not in the general literary history of his age, at least in the particular history of the science which he teaches. It will presently be seen that the author of "English Grammar in Familiar Lectures," boasts of a degree of success and popularity, which, in this age of the world, has no parallel. It is not intended on my part, to dispute any of his assertions on these points; but rather to take it for granted, that in reputation and revenue he is altogether as preëminent as he pretends to be. The character of his alleged *improvements*, however, I shall inspect with the eyes of one who means to know the certainty for himself; and, in this item of literary history, the reader shall see, in some sort, *what profit* there is in grammar.

25. Take first from one page of his "hundred and fifth edition," a few brief quotations, as a sample of his thoughts and style:

"They, however, who introduce *usages which depart from the analogy and philosophy* of a language, *are conspicuous* among the number of those who *form that language,* and have power to control it." "PRINCIPLE.—A principle in grammar is a *peculiar construction* of the language, sanctioned by good usage." "DEFINITION.—A definition in grammar is a *principle* of language expressed in a *definite form.*" "RULE.—A rule describes *the peculiar construction* or circumstantial relation of words, *which* custom has established for our observance."—*Kirkham's Grammar,* page 18.

Now, as "a rule describes a peculiar construction," and "a principle is a peculiar construction," and "a definition is a principle;" how, according to this grammarian, do a principle, a definition, and a rule, differ each from the others? From the rote here imposed, it is certainly not easier for the learner to conceive of all these things *distinctly,* than it is to understand how a departure from philosophy may make a man deservedly "*conspicuous.*" It were easy to multiply examples like these, showing the work to be deficient in clearness, the first requisite of style.

26. The following passages may serve as a specimen of the gentleman's taste, and grammatical accuracy; in one of which, he supposes the neuter verb *is* to express an *action,* and every *honest man* to be *long since dead!* So it stands in all his editions. Did his praisers think so too?

"It is correct to say, *The man eats, he eats*; but we cannot say, *The man dog eats, he dog eats.* Why not? Because the man *is here represented* as the possessor, and dog, the property, or thing possessed; and the genius of our language requires, that when we add *to the possessor,* the *thing* which *he* is represented as possessing, *the possessor* shall take a particular form to show ITS case, or relation to the property."—*Ib.*, p. 52.

THE PRESENT TENSE.—"This tense is sometimes applied to represent the *actions* of persons *long since dead*; as, 'Seneca *reasons* and *moralizes* well; An HONEST MAN IS the noblest work of God.'"—*Ib.*, p. 138.

PARTICIPLES.—"The term *Participle* comes from the Latin word *participio*,[10] which signifies to *partake*."—"Participles are formed by adding to the verb the termination *ing, ed*, or *en. Ing* signifies the same thing as the noun *being*. When *postfixed* to the *noun-state* of the verb, the *compound word* thus formed expresses a continued state of the *verbal denotement*. It implies that what is meant by the verb, is *being* continued."—*Ib.*, p. 78. "All participles *are compound* in their meaning and office."—*Ib.*, p. 79.

VERBS.—"Verbs express, not only *the state* or *manner of being*, but, likewise, all the different *actions* and *movements* of all creatures and things, whether animate or inanimate."—*Ib.*, p. 62. "It can be easily shown, that from the noun and verb, all the other parts of speech have sprung. Nay, more. *They* may even be reduced to *one. Verbs do not, in reality, express actions*; but they are intrinsically *the mere* NAMES *of actions*."—*Ib.*, p. 37.

PHILOSOPHICAL GRAMMAR.—"I have thought proper to intersperse through the pages of this work, under the head of '*Philosophical Notes*,' an entire system of grammatical principles, as deduced from what *appears*[11] *to me* to be the *most rational and consistent* philosophical investigations."— *Ib.*, p. 36. "Johnson, and Blair, and Lowth, *would have been laughed at*, had they essayed to thrust *any thing like our* modernized philosophical grammar *down the throats of their cotemporaries*."—*Ib.*, p. 143.

Is it not a pity, that "more than one hundred thousand children and youth" should be daily poring over language and logic like this?

27. For the sake of those who happily remain ignorant of this successful empiricism, it is desirable that the record and exposition of it be made brief. There is little danger that it will long survive its author. But the present subjects of it are sufficiently numerous to deserve some pity. The following is a sample of the gentleman's method of achieving what he both justly and exultingly supposes, that Johnson, or Blair, or Lowth, could not have effected. He scoffs at his own grave instructions, as if they had been the production of some *other* impostor. Can the fact be credited, that in the following instances, he speaks of *what he himself teaches?*—of what he seriously pronounces *"most rational and consistent?"*—of what is part and parcel of that philosophy of his, which he declares, "will *in general be found to accord* with the *practical theory* embraced in the body of his work?"—See *Kirkham's Gram.*, p. 36.

"Call this '*philosophical parsing,* on reasoning principles, according to the original laws of nature and of thought,' and *the pill will be swallowed,* by pedants and their dupes, with the greatest ease imaginable."—*Kirkham's Gram.*, p. 144. "For the *satisfaction* of those teachers who prefer it, and *for their adoption, too,* a modernized philosophical theory of the moods and tenses is here presented. If it is not quite so convenient and useful as the old one, they need not hesitate to adopt it. It has the advantage of being *new*; and, moreover, it sounds *large*, and will make the *commonalty stare*. Let it be distinctly understood that you teach '[*Kirkham's*] *philosophical grammar,* founded on reason and common sense,' and you will pass for a very learned man, and make all the good housewives wonder at the rapid march of intellect, and the vast improvements of the age."—*Ib.*, p. 141.

28. The *pretty promises* with which these "Familiar Lectures" abound, are also worthy to be noticed here, as being among the peculiar attractions of the performance. The following may serve as a specimen:

"If you *proceed according to my instructions*, you will be sure to acquire a practical knowledge of Grammar in *a short time.*"—Kirkham's Gram., p. 49. "If you have sufficient *resolution to do this*, you will, in a short time, *perfectly understand* the nature and office of the different parts of speech, their various properties and relations, and the rules of syntax that apply to them; *and, in a few weeks*, be able to speak and write accurately."—Ib., p. 62. "You will please to turn back and read over again *the whole five lectures*. You must exercise *a little* patience."—Ib., p. 82. "By studying these lectures with attention, you will acquire *more grammatical* knowledge in three months, than is commonly obtained in *two years.*"—Ib., p. 82. "I will conduct you *so smoothly through the moods and tenses*, and the conjugation of verbs, that, instead of finding yourself involved in obscurities and deep intricacies, you will scarcely find *an obstruction to impede your progress.*"—Ib., p. 133. "The supposed Herculean task of learning to conjugate verbs, will be transformed into *a few hours of pleasant pastime.*"—Ib., p. 142. "*By examining carefully* the conjugation of the verb through this mood, you will find it *very easy.*"—Ib., p. 147. "By pursuing the following direction, you can, *in a very short time*, learn to conjugate any verb."—Ib., p. 147. "Although this mode of procedure *may, at first, appear to be laborious*, yet, as it is necessary, I trust you will not hesitate to adopt it. *My confidence in your perseverance*, induces me to recommend *any course* which I know will tend to facilitate your progress."—Ib., p. 148.

29. The grand boast of this author is, that he *has succeeded* in "pleasing himself and the public." He trusts to have "gained the latter point," to so great an extent, and with such security of tenure, that henceforth no man

can safely question *the merit* of his performance. Happy mortal! to whom that success which is the ground of his pride, is also the glittering ægis of his sure defence! To this he points with exultation and self-applause, as if the prosperity of the wicked, or the popularity of an imposture, had never yet been heard of in this clever world![12] Upon what merit this success has been founded, my readers may judge, when I shall have finished this slight review of his work. Probably no other grammar was ever so industriously spread. Such was the author's perseverance in his measures to increase the demand for his book, that even the attainment of such accuracy as he was capable of, was less a subject of concern. For in an article designed "to ward off some of the arrows of criticism,"—an advertisement which, from the eleventh to the "one hundred and fifth edition," has been promising "to the *publick another and a better* edition,"—he plainly offers this urgent engagement, as "an apology for its defects:"

"The author is apprehensive that his work is *not yet as* accurate and as much simplified as it *may be.* If, however, the disadvantages of lingering under a broken constitution, and of being able to devote to this subject *only a small portion of his time,* snatched from the *active pursuits of a business life,* (active as far as imperfect health permits him to be,) are any apology for his defects, he hopes that the candid will set down *the apology to his credit.*—Not that he would beg a truce with the gentlemen *criticks* and reviewers. Any compromise with them would betray a want of *self-confidence* and *moral courage,* which he would by no means, be willing to avow."—*Kirkham's Gram.*, (Adv. of 1829,) p. 7.

30. Now, to this painful struggle, this active contention between business and the vapours, let all *credit* be given, and all *sympathy* be added; but, as an aid to the studies of healthy children, what better is the book, for any forbearance or favour that may have been won by this apology? It is well known, that, till *phrenology* became the common talk, the author's principal

business was, to commend his own method of teaching *grammar*, and to turn this publication to profit. This honourable industry, aided, as himself suggests, by "not much *less* than one thousand written recommendations," is said to have wrought for him, in a very few years, a degree of success and fame, at which both the eulogists of Murray and the friends of English grammar may hang their heads. As to a "*compromise*" with any critic or reviewer whom he cannot bribe, it is enough to say of that, it is morally impossible. Nor was it necessary for such an author to throw the gauntlet, to prove himself not lacking in "*self-confidence.*" He can show his "*moral courage,*" only by daring do right.

31. In 1829, after his book had gone through ten editions, and the demand for it had become so great as "to call forth twenty thousand copies during the year," the prudent author, intending to veer his course according to the *trade-wind*, thought it expedient to retract his former acknowledgement to "our best modern philologists," and to profess himself a modifier of the Great Compiler's code. Where then holds the anchor of his praise? Let the reader say, after weighing and comparing his various pretensions:

"Aware that there is, in the *publick* mind, a strong predilection for the doctrines contained in Mr. Murray's grammar, he has thought proper, not merely from motives of policy, but from choice, *to select his principles chiefly from that work*; and, moreover, to adopt, as far as consistent with his own views, *the language of that eminent philologist.* In no instance has he varied from him, unless he conceived that, in so doing, *some practical advantage* would be gained. He hopes, *therefore,* to escape the censure so frequently and so justly awarded to those *unfortunate innovators* who have not scrupled to alter, mutilate, and torture the text of that able writer, merely to gratify an itching propensity to figure in the world *as authors*, and gain an ephemeral popularity by arrogating to themselves *the credit due to another.*" [13]—*Kirkham's Gram.*, 1829, p. 10.

32. Now these statements are either true or false; and I know not on which supposition they are most creditable to the writer. Had any Roman grammatist thus profited by the name of Varro or Quintilian, he would have been filled with constant dread of somewhere meeting the injured author's frowning shade! Surely, among the professed admirers of Murray, no other man, whether innovator or copyist, unfortunate or successful, is at all to be compared to this gentleman for the audacity with which he has "not scrupled to alter, mutilate, and torture, the text of that able writer." Murray simply intended to do good, and good that might descend to posterity; and this just and generous intention goes far to excuse even his errors. But Kirkham, speaking of posterity, scruples not to disavow and to renounce all care for them, or for any thing which a coming age may think of his character: saying,

"My pretensions reach not so far. To the *present generation only*, I present my claims. Should it lend me a listening ear, and grant me its suffrages, *the height of my ambition* will be attained."—*Advertisement, in his Elocution*, p. 346.

His whole design is, therefore, upon the very face of it, a paltry scheme of present income. And, seeing his entered classes of boys and girls must soon have done with him, he has doubtless acted wisely, and quite in accordance with his own interest, to have made all possible haste in his career.

33. Being no rival with him in this race, and having no personal quarrel with him on any account, I would, for his sake, fain rejoice at his success, and withhold my criticisms; because he is said to have been liberal with his gains, and because he has not, like some others, copied me instead of

Murray. But the vindication of a greatly injured and perverted science, constrains me to say, on this occasion, that pretensions less consistent with themselves, or less sustained by taste and scholarship, have seldom, if ever, been promulgated in the name of grammar. I have, certainly, no intention to say more than is due to the uninformed and misguided. For some who are ungenerous and prejudiced themselves, will not be unwilling to think me so; and even this freedom, backed and guarded as it is by facts and proofs irrefragable, may still be ingeniously ascribed to an ill motive. To two thirds of the community, one grammar is just as good as an other; because they neither know, nor wish to know, more than may be learned from the very worst. An honest expression of sentiment against abuses of a literary nature, is little the fashion of these times; and the good people who purchase books upon the recommendations of others, may be slow to believe there is no merit where so much has been attributed. But facts may well be credited, in opposition to courteous flattery, when there are the author's own words and works to vouch for them in the face of day. Though a thousand of our great men may have helped a copier's weak copyist to take "some practical advantage" of the world's credulity, it is safe to aver, in the face of dignity still greater, that testimonials more fallacious have seldom mocked the cause of learning. They did not read his book.

34. Notwithstanding the author's change in his professions, the work is now essentially the same as it was at first; except that its errors and contradictions have been greatly multiplied, by the addition of new matter inconsistent with the old. He evidently cares not what doctrines he teaches, or whose; but, as various theories are noised abroad, seizes upon different opinions, and mixes them together, that his books may contain something to suit all parties. "*A System of Philosophical Grammar*," though but an idle speculation, even in his own account, and doubly absurd in him, as being flatly contradictory to his main text, has been thought worthy of insertion. And what his title-page denominates "*A New System of Punctuation*,"

though mostly in the very words of Murray, was next invented to supply a deficiency which he at length discovered. To admit these, and some other additions, the "comprehensive system-of grammar" was gradually extended from 144 small duodecimo pages, to 228 of the ordinary size. And, in this compass, it was finally stereotyped in 1829; so that the ninety-four editions published since, have nothing new for history.

35. But the publication of an other work designed for schools, "*An Essay an Elocution*" shows the progress of the author's mind. Nothing can be more radically opposite, than are some of the elementary doctrines which this gentleman is now teaching; nothing, more strangely inconsistent, than are some of his declarations and professions. For instance: "A consonant is a letter that cannot be perfectly sounded without the help of a vowel."—*Kirkham's Gram.*, p. 19. Again: "A consonant is not only capable of being perfectly sounded without the help of a vowel, but, moreover, of forming, like a vowel, a separate syllable."—*Kirkham's Elocution*, p. 32. Take a second example. He makes "ADJECTIVE PRONOUNS" a *prominent division* and *leading title*, in treating of the pronouns proper; defines the term in a manner peculiar to himself; prefers and uses it in all his parsing; and yet, by the third sentence of the story, the learner is conducted to this just conclusion: "Hence, such a thing as an *adjective-pronoun* cannot exist."—*Grammar*, p. 105. Once more. Upon his own rules, or such as he had borrowed, he comments thus, and comments *truly*, because he had either written them badly or made an ill choice: "But some of these rules are foolish, trifling, and unimportant."—*Elocution*, p. 97. Again: "Rules 10 and 11, rest on a sandy foundation. They appear not to be based on the principles of the language."—*Grammar*, p. 59. These are but specimens of his own frequent testimony against himself! Nor shall he find refuge in the impudent falsehood, that the things which I quote as his, are not his own. [14] These contradictory texts, and scores of others which might be added to them, are as rightfully his own, as any doctrine he has ever yet

inculcated. But, upon the credulity of ignorance, his high-sounding certificates and unbounded boasting can impose any thing. They overrule all in favour of cue of the worst grammars extant;—of which he says, "it is now studied by more than one hundred thousand children and youth; and is more extensively used than *all other English grammars* published in the United States."—*Elocution*, p. 347. The booksellers say, he receives from his publishers *ten cents a copy*, on this work, and that he reports the sale of *sixty thousand copies per annum*. Such has of late been his public boast. I have once had the story from his own lips, and of course congratulated him, though I dislike the book. Six thousand dollars a year, on this most miserable modification of Lindley Murray's Grammar! Be it so—or double, if he and the public please. Murray had so little originality in his work, or so little selfishness in his design, that he would not take any thing; and his may ultimately prove the better bargain.

36. A man may boast and bless himself as he pleases, his fortune, surely, can never be worthy of an other's envy, so long as he finds it inadequate to his own great merits, and unworthy of his own poor gratitude. As a grammarian, Kirkham claims to be second only to Lindley Murray; and says, "Since the days of Lowth, no other work on grammar, Murray's only excepted, has been so favourably received by the *publick* as his own. As a proof of this, he would mention, that within the last six years it has passed through *fifty* editions."—*Preface to Elocution*, p. 12. And, at the same time, and in the same preface, he complains, that, "Of all the labours done under the sun, the labours *of the pen* meet with the poorest reward."—*Ibid.*, p. 5. This too clearly favours the report, that his books were not written by himself, but by others whom he hired. Possibly, the anonymous helper may here have penned, not his employer's feeling, but a line of his own experience. But I choose to ascribe the passage to the professed author, and to hold him answerable for the inconsistency. Willing to illustrate by the best and fairest examples these fruitful means of grammatical fame, I am

glad of his present success, which, through this record, shall become yet more famous. It is the only thing which makes him worthy of the notice here taken of him. But I cannot sympathize with his complaint, because he never sought any but "the poorest reward;" and more than all he sought, he found. In his last "Address to Teachers," he says, "He may doubtless be permitted emphatically to say with Prospero, '*Your breath has filled my sails.*'"—*Elocution*, p. 18. If this boasting has any truth in it, he ought to be satisfied. But it is written, "He that loveth silver, shall not be satisfied with silver; nor he that loveth abundance, with increase." Let him remember this. [15] He now announces three or four other works as forthcoming shortly. What these will achieve, the world will see. But I must confine myself to the Grammar.

37. In this volume, scarcely any thing is found where it might be expected. "The author," as he tells us in his preface, "has not followed the common 'artificial and unnatural arrangement adopted by most of his predecessors;' *yet he* has endeavoured to pursue a more judicious one, namely, '*the order of the understanding.*'"—*Grammar*, p. 12. But if this is the order of his understanding, he is greatly to be pitied. A book more confused in its plan, more wanting in method, more imperfect in distinctness of parts, more deficient in symmetry, or more difficult of reference, shall not easily be found in stereotype. Let the reader try to follow us here. Bating twelve pages at the beginning, occupied by the title, recommendations, advertisement, contents, preface, hints to teachers, and advice to lecturers; and fifty-four at the end, embracing syntax, orthography, orthoëpy, provincialisms, prosody, punctuation, versification, rhetoric, figures of speech, and a Key, all in the sequence here given; the work consists of fourteen chapters of grammar, absurdly called "Familiar Lectures." The first treats of sundries, under half a dozen titles, but chiefly of Orthography; and the last is three pages and a half, of the most common remarks, on Derivation. In the remaining twelve, the Etymology and Syntax

of the ten parts of speech are commingled; and an attempt is made, to teach simultaneously all that the author judged important in either. Hence he gives us, in a strange congeries, rules, remarks, illustrations, false syntax, systematic parsing, exercises in parsing, two different orders of notes, three different orders of questions, and a variety of other titles merely occasional. All these things, being additional to his main text, are to be connected, in the mind of the learner, with the parts of speech successively, in some new and inexplicable catenation found only in the arrangement of the lectures. The author himself could not see through the chaos. He accordingly made his table of contents a mere meagre alphabetical index. Having once attempted in vain to explain the order of his instructions, he actually gave the matter up in despair!

38. In length, these pretended lectures vary, from three or four pages, to eight-and-thirty. Their subjects run thus: 1. Language, Grammar, Orthography; 2. Nouns and Verbs; 3. Articles; 4. Adjectives; 5. Participles; 6. Adverbs; 7. Prepositions; 8. Pronouns; 9. Conjunctions; 10. Interjections and Nouns; 11. Moods and Tenses; 12. Irregular Verbs; 13. Auxiliary, Passive, and Defective Verbs; 14. Derivation. Which, now, is "more judicious," such confusion as this, or the arrangement which has been common from time immemorial? Who that has any respect for the human intellect, or whose powers of mind deserve any in return, will avouch this jumble to be "the order of the understanding?" Are the methods of science to be accounted mere hinderances to instruction? Has grammar really been made easy by this confounding of its parts? Or are we lured by the name, *Familiar Lectures*,"—a term manifestly adopted as a mere decoy, and, with respect to the work itself, totally inappropriate? If these chapters have ever been actually delivered as a series of lectures, the reader must have been employed on some occasions eight or ten times as long as on others! "People," says Dr. Johnson, "have now-a-days got a strange opinion that every thing should be taught by *lectures*. Now, I cannot see that lectures can

do so much good as a private reading of the books from which the lectures are taken. I know of nothing that can be best taught by lectures, except where experiments are to be shown. You may teach chymistry by lectures—you *might* teach the making of shoes by lectures." —*Boswell's Life of Johnson.*

39. With singular ignorance and untruth, this gentleman claims to have invented a better method of analysis than had ever been practised before. Of other grammars, his preface avers, "They have *all overlooked* what the author considers a very important object; namely, *a systematick order of parsing.*"—*Grammar*, p. 9. And, in his "Hints to Teachers," presenting himself as a model, and his book as a paragon, he says: "By pursuing this system, he can, with less labour, advance a pupil *farther* in the practical knowledge of this *abstruse science*, in *two months*, than he could in *one year*, when he taught in the *old way*."—*Grammar*, p. 12. What his "*old way*" was, does not appear. Doubtless something sufficiently bad. And as to his new way, I shall hereafter have occasion to show that *that* is sufficiently bad also. But to this gasconade the simple-minded have given credit—because the author showed certificates that testified to his great success, and called him "amiable and modest!" But who can look into the book, or into the writer's pretensions in regard to his predecessors, and conceive the merit which has made him—"preëminent by so much odds?" Was Murray less praiseworthy, less amiable, or less modest? In illustration of my topic, and for the sake of literary justice, I have selected that honoured "*Compiler*" to show the abuses of praise; let the history of this his vaunting *modifier* cap the climax of vanity. In general, his amendments of "that eminent philologist," are not more skillful than the following touch upon an eminent dramatist; and here, it is plain, he has mistaken two nouns for adjectives, and converted into bad English a beautiful passage, the sentiment of which is worthy of an *author's* recollection:

"The evil *deed* or *deeds* that men do, *lives* after them;
The good *deed* or *deeds is* oft interred with their bones." [16]
Kirkham's Grammar, p. 75.

40. Lord Bacon observes, "Nothing is thought so easy a request to a great person as his letter; and yet, if it be not in a good cause, it is so much out of his reputation." It is to this mischievous facility of recommendation, this prostituted influence of great names, that the inconvenient diversity of school-books, and the continued use of bad ones, are in a great measure to be attributed. It belongs to those who understand the subjects of which authors profess to treat, to judge fairly and fully of their works, and then to let the *reasons* of their judgement be known. For no one will question the fact, that a vast number of the school-books now in use are either egregious plagiarisms or productions of no comparative merit. And, what is still more surprising and monstrous, presidents, governors, senators, and judges; professors, doctors, clergymen, and lawyers; a host of titled connoisseurs; with incredible facility lend their names, not only to works of inferior merit, but to the vilest thefts, and the wildest absurdities, palmed off upon their own and the public credulity, under pretence of improvement. The man who thus prefixes his letter of recommendation to an ill-written book, publishes, out of mere courtesy, a direct impeachment of his own scholarship or integrity. Yet, how often have we seen the honours of a high office, or even of a worthy name, prostituted to give a temporary or local currency to a book which it would disgrace any man of letters to quote! With such encouragement, nonsense wrestles for the seat of learning, exploded errors are republished as novelties, original writers are plundered by dunces, and men that understand nothing well, profess to teach all sciences!

41. All praise of excellence must needs be comparative, because the thing itself is so. To excel in grammar, is but to know better than others wherein grammatical excellence consists. Hence there is no fixed point of perfection

beyond which such learning may not be carried. The limit to improvement is not so much in the nature of the subject, as in the powers of the mind, and in the inducements to exert them upon a theme so humble and so uninviting. Dr. Johnson suggests, in his masterly preface, "that a whole life cannot be spent upon syntax and etymology, and that even a whole life would not be sufficient." Who then will suppose, in the face of such facts and confessions as have been exhibited, that either in the faulty publications of Murray, or among the various modifications of them by other hands we have any such work as deserves to be made a permanent standard of instruction in English grammar? With great sacrifices, both of pleasure and of interest, I have humbly endeavoured to supply this desideratum; and it remains for other men to determine, and other times to know, what place shall be given to these my labours, in the general story of this branch of learning. Intending to develop not only the principles but also the history of grammar, I could not but speak of its authors. The writer who looks broadly at the past and the present, to give sound instruction to the future, must not judge of men by their shadows. If the truth, honestly told, diminish the stature of some, it does it merely by clearing the sight of the beholder. Real greatness cannot suffer loss by the dissipating of a vapour. If reputation has been raised upon the mist of ignorance, who but the builder shall lament its overthrow? If the works of grammarians are often ungrammatical, whose fault is this but their own? If *all* grammatical fame is little in itself, how can the abatement of what is undeserved of it be much? If the errors of some have long been tolerated, what right of the critic has been lost by nonuser? If the interests of Science have been sacrificed to Mammon, what rebuke can do injustice to the craft? Nay, let the broad-axe of the critic hew up to the line, till every beam in her temple be smooth and straight. For, "certainly, next to commending good writers, the greatest service to learning is, to expose the bad, who can only in that way be made of any use to it." [17] And if, among the makers of grammars, the scribblings of some, and the filchings of others, are discreditable alike to themselves and to their theme, let the reader consider, how great must be the intrinsic worth of that study which still maintains its credit in spite of all these abuses!

CHAPTER IV.

OF THE ORIGIN OF LANGUAGE.

"Tot fallaciis obrutum, tot hallucinationibus demersum, tot adhuc tenebris circumfusum studium hocce mihi visum est, ut nihil satis tuto in hac materia præstari posse arbitratus sim, nisi nova quadam arte critica præmissa."—SCIPIO MAFFEIUS: *Cassiod. Complexiones*, p. xxx.

1. The origin of things is, for many reasons, a peculiarly interesting point in their history. Among those who have thought fit to inquire into the prime origin of speech, it has been matter of dispute, whether we ought to consider it a special gift from Heaven, or an acquisition of industry—a natural endowment, or an artificial invention. Nor is any thing that has ever yet been said upon it, sufficient to set the question permanently at rest. That there is in some words, and perhaps in some of every language, a natural connexion between the sounds uttered and the things signified, cannot be denied; yet, on the other hand, there is, in the use of words in general, so much to which nature affords no clew or index, that this whole process of communicating thought by speech, seems to be artificial. Under an other head, I have already cited from Sanctius some opinions of the ancient grammarians and philosophers on this point. With the reasoning of that zealous instructor, the following sentence from Dr. Blair very obviously accords: "To suppose words invented, or names given to things, in a manner purely arbitrary, without any ground or reason, is to suppose an effect

without a cause. There must have always been some motive which led to the assignation of one name rather than an other."—*Rhet.*, Lect. vi, p. 55.

2. But, in their endeavours to explain the origin and early progress of language, several learned men, among whom is this celebrated lecturer, have needlessly perplexed both themselves and their readers, with sundry questions, assumptions, and reasonings, which are manifestly contrary to what has been made known to us on the best of all authority. What signifies it[18] for a man to tell us how nations rude and barbarous invented interjections first,[19] and then nouns, and then verbs,[20] and finally the other parts of speech; when he himself confesses that he does not know whether language "can be considered a human invention at all;" and when he believed, or ought to have believed, that the speech of the first man, though probably augmented by those who afterwards used it, was, essentially, the one language of the earth for more than eighteen centuries? The task of inventing a language *de novo*, could surely have fallen upon no man but Adam; and he, in the garden of Paradise, had doubtless some aids and facilities not common to every wild man of the woods.

3. The learned Doctor was equally puzzled to conceive, "either how society could form itself, previously to language, or how words could rise into a language, previously to society formed."—*Blair's Rhet.*, Lect. vi, p. 54. This too was but an idle perplexity, though thousands have gravely pored over it since, as a part of the study of rhetoric; for, if neither could be previous to the other, they must have sprung up simultaneously. And it is a sort of slander upon our prime ancestor, to suggest, that, because he was "*the first*," he must have been "*the rudest*" of his race; and that, "consequently, those first rudiments of speech," which alone the supposition allows to him or to his family, "must have been poor and narrow."—*Blair's Rhet.*, p. 54. It is far more reasonable to think, with a later author, that, "Adam had an insight into natural things far beyond the acutest philosopher,

as may be gathered from his giving of names to all creatures, according to their different constitutions."—*Robinson's Scripture Characters*, p. 4.

4. But Dr. Blair is not alone in the view which he here takes. The same thing has bean suggested by other learned men. Thus Dr. James P. Wilson, of Philadelphia, in an octavo published in 1817, says: "It is difficult to discern how communities could have existed without language, and equally so to discover how language could have obtained, in a peopled world, prior to society."—*Wilson's Essay on Gram.*, p. 1. I know not how so many professed Christians, and some of them teachers of religion too, with the Bible in their hands, can reason upon this subject as they do. We find them, in their speculations, conspiring to represent primeval man, to use their own words, as a "*savage*, whose 'howl at the appearance of danger, and whose exclamations of joy at the sight of his prey, reiterated, or varied with the change of objects, were probably the origin of language.'—*Booth's Analytical Dictionary*. In the dawn of society, ages may have passed away, with little more converse than what these efforts would produce."—*Gardiner's Music of Nature*, p. 31. Here Gardiner quotes Booth with approbation, and the latter, like Wilson, may have borrowed his ideas from Blair. Thus are we taught by a multitude of guessers, grave, learned, and oracular, that the last of the ten parts of speech was in fact the first: "*Interjections* are exceedingly interesting in one respect. They are, there can be little doubt, *the oldest words* in all languages; and may be considered the elements of speech."—*Bucke's Classical Gram.*, p. 78. On this point, however, Dr. Blair seems not to be quite consistent with himself: "Those exclamations, therefore, which by grammarians are called *interjections*, uttered in a strong and passionate manner, were, *beyond doubt*, the first elements or beginnings of speech."—*Rhet.*, Lect. vi, p. 55. "The *names* of sensible objects were, *in all languages*, the words most early introduced."—*Rhet.*, Lect. xiv, p. 135. "The *names of sensible objects*," says Murray too,

"were the words most early introduced."—*Octavo Gram.*, p. 336. Bat what says the Bible?

5. Revelation informs us that our first progenitor was not only endowed with the faculty of speech, but, as it would appear, actually incited by the Deity to exert that faculty in giving *names* to the objects by which he was surrounded. "Out of the ground the Lord God formed every beast of the field and every fowl of the air; and brought them unto Adam, to see what he would call them: and whatsoever Adam called every living creature, that was the name thereof. And Adam gave names to all cattle, and to the fowls of the air, and to every beast of the field; but for Adam there was not found a help meet for him."—*Gen.*, ii, 19, 20. This account of the first naming of the other creatures by man, is apparently a parenthesis in the story of the creation of woman, with which the second chapter of Genesis concludes. But, in the preceding chapter, the Deity is represented not only as calling all things into existence *by his Word*; but as *speaking to the first human pair*, with reference to their increase in the earth, and to their dominion over it, and over all the living creatures formed to inhabit it. So that the order of the events cannot be clearly inferred from the order of the narration. The manner of this communication to man, may also be a subject of doubt. Whether it was, or was not, made by a voice of words, may be questioned. But, surely, that Being who, in creating the world and its inhabitants, manifested his own infinite wisdom, eternal power, and godhead, does not lack words, or any other means of signification, if he will use them. And, in the inspired record of his work in the beginning, he is certainly represented, not only as naming all things imperatively, when he spoke them into being, but as expressly calling the light *Day*, the darkness *Night*, the firmament *Heaven*, the dry land *Earth*, and the gatherings of the mighty waters *Seas*.

6. Dr. Thomas Hartwell Horne, in commending a work by Dr. Ellis, concerning the origin of human wisdom and understanding, says: "It shows

satisfactorily, that religion *and language* entered the world by divine revelation, without the aid of which, man had not been a rational or religious creature."—*Study of the Scriptures,* Vol. i, p. 4. "Plato attributes the primitive words of the *first language* to a divine origin;" and Dr. Wilson remarks, "The transition from silence to speech, implies an effort of the understanding too great for man."—*Essay on Gram.*, p. 1. Dr. Beattie says, "Mankind must have spoken in all ages, the young constantly learning to speak by imitating those who were older; and, if so, our first parents must have received this art, as well as some others, by inspiration."—*Moral Science*, p. 27. Horne Tooke says, "I imagine that it is, *in some measure*, with the vehicle of our thoughts, as with the vehicles for our bodies. Necessity produced both."—*Diversions of Purley*, Vol. i, p. 20. Again: "Language, it is true, *is an art*, and a glorious one; whose influence extends over all the others, and in which finally all science whatever must centre: but an art *springing from necessity*, and originally invented by artless men, who did not sit down like philosophers to invent it."—*Ib.*, Vol. i, p. 259.

7. Milton imagines Adam's first knowledge of speech, to have sprung from the hearing of his own voice; and that voice to have been raised, instinctively, or spontaneously, in an animated inquiry concerning his own origin—an inquiry in which he addresses to unintelligent objects, and inferior creatures, such questions as the Deity alone could answer:

"Myself I then perused, and limb by limb
Surveyed, and sometimes went, and sometimes ran
With supple joints, as lively vigor led:
But who I was, or where, or from what cause,
Knew not; *to speak I tried, and forthwith spake;
My tongue obeyed, and readily could name
Whatever I saw.* 'Thou Sun,' said I, 'fair light,
And thou enlightened Earth, so fresh and gay,

> Ye Hills and Dales, ye Rivers, Woods, and Plains;
> And ye that live and move, fair Creatures! tell,
> Tell, if ye saw, how came I thus, how here?
> Not of myself; by some great Maker then,
> In goodness and in power preëminent:
> Tell me how I may know him, how adore,
> From whom I have that thus I move and live,
> And feel that I am happier than I know.'"
>   *Paradise Lost*, Book viii, l. 267.

But, to the imagination of a poet, a freedom is allowed, which belongs not to philosophy. We have not always the means of knowing how far he *literally* believes what he states.

8. My own opinion is, that language is partly natural and partly artificial. And, as the following quotation from the Greek of Ammonius will serve in some degree to illustrate it, I present the passage in English for the consideration of those who may prefer ancient to modern speculations: "In the same manner, therefore, as mere motion is from nature, but dancing is something positive; and as wood exists in nature, but a door is something positive; so is the mere utterance of vocal sound founded in nature, but the signification of ideas by nouns or verbs is something positive. And hence it is, that, as to the simple power of producing vocal sound—which is as it were the organ or instrument of the soul's faculties of knowledge or volition—as to this vocal power, I say, man seems to possess it from nature, in like manner as irrational animals; but as to the power of using significantly nouns or verbs, or sentences combining these, (which are not natural but positive,) this he possesses by way of peculiar eminence; because he alone of all mortal beings partakes of a soul which can move itself, and operate to the production of arts. So that, even in the utterance of sounds, the inventive power of the mind is discerned; as the various elegant compositions, both in

metre, and without metre, abundantly prove."—*Ammon. de Interpr.*, p. 51. [21]

9. Man was made for society; and from the first period of human existence the race were social. Monkish seclusion is manifestly unnatural; and the wild independence of the savage, is properly denominated a state of nature, only in contradistinction to that state in which the arts are cultivated. But to civilized life, or even to that which is in any degree social, language is absolutely necessary. There is therefore no danger that the language of any nation shall fall into disuse, till the people by whom it is spoken, shall either adopt some other, or become themselves extinct. When the latter event occurs, as is the case with the ancient Hebrew, Greek, and Latin, the language, if preserved at all from oblivion, becomes the more permanent; because the causes which are constantly tending to improve or deteriorate every living language, have ceased to operate upon those which are learned only from ancient books. The inflections which now compose the declensions and conjugations of the dead languages, and which indeed have ever constituted the peculiar characteristics of those forms of speech, must remain forever as they are.

10. When a nation changes, its language, as did our forefathers in Britain, producing by a gradual amalgamation of materials drawn from various tongues a new one differing from all, the first stages of its grammar will of course be chaotic and rude. Uniformity springs from the steady application of rules; and polish is the work of taste and refinement. We may easily err by following the example of our early writers with more reverence than judgement; nor is it possible for us to do justice to the grammarians, whether early or late, without a knowledge both of the history and of the present state of the science which they profess to teach. I therefore think it proper rapidly to glance at many things remote indeed in time, yet nearer to my present purpose, and abundantly more worthy of the student's

consideration, than a thousand matters which are taught for grammar by the authors of treatises professedly elementary.

11. As we have already seen, some have supposed that the formation of the first language must have been very slow and gradual. But of this they offer no proof, and from the pen of inspiration we seem to have testimony against it. Did Adam give names to all the creatures about him, and then allow those names to be immediately forgotten? Did not both he and his family continually use his original nouns in their social intercourse? and how could they use them, without other parts of speech to form them into sentences? Nay, do we not know from the Bible, that on several occasions our prime ancestor expressed himself like an intelligent man, and used all the parts of speech which are now considered *necessary*? What did he say, when his fit partner, the fairest and loveliest work of God, was presented to him? "This is now bone of my bones, and flesh of my flesh: she shall be called Woman, because she was taken out of Man." And again: Had he not other words than nouns, when he made answer concerning his transgression: "I heard thy voice in the garden, and I was afraid, because I was naked; and I hid myself?" What is it, then, but a groundless assumption, to make him and his immediate descendants ignorant savages, and to affirm, with Dr. Blair, that "their speech must have been poor and narrow?" It is not possible now to ascertan what degree of perfection the oral communication of the first age exhibited. But, as languages are now known to improve in proportion to the improvement of society in civilization and intelligence, and as we cannot reasonably suppose the first inhabitants of the earth to have been savages, it seems, I think, a plausible conjecture, that the primeval tongue was at least sufficient for all the ordinary intercourse of civilized men, living in the simple manner ascribed to our early ancestors in Scripture; and that, in many instances, human speech subsequently declined far below its original standard.

12. At any rate, let it be remembered that the first language spoken on earth, whatever it was, originated in Eden before the fall; that this "one language," which all men understood until the dispersion, is to be traced, not to the cries of savage hunters, echoed through the wilds and glades where Nimrod planted Babel, but to that eastern garden of God's own planting, wherein grew "every tree that is pleasant to the sight and good for food;" to that paradise into which the Lord God put the new-created man, "to dress it and to keep it." It was here that Adam and his partner learned to speak, while yet they stood blameless and blessed, entire and wanting nothing; free in the exercise of perfect faculties of body and mind, capable of acquiring knowledge through observation and experience, and also favoured with immediate communications with their Maker. Yet Adam, having nothing which he did not receive, could not originally bring any real knowledge into the world with him, any more than men do now: this, in whatever degree attained, must be, and must always have been, either an acquisition of reason, or a revelation from God. And, according to the understanding of some, even in the beginning, "That was not first which is spiritual, but that which is natural; and afterward that which is spiritual."—*1 Cor., xv, 46.* That is, the spirit of Christ, the second Adam, was bestowed on the first Adam, after his creation, as the life and the light of the immortal soul. For, "In *Him* was life, and the life was the light of men," a life which our first parents forfeited and lost on the day of their transgression. "It was undoubtedly in the light of this pure influence that Adam had such an intuitive discerning of the creation, as enabled him to give names to all creatures according to their several natures."—*Phipps, on Man,* p. 4. A lapse from all this favour, into conscious guilt and misery; a knowledge of good withdrawn, and of evil made too sure; followed the first transgression. Abandoned then in great measure by superhuman aid, and left to contend with foes without and foes within, mankind became what history and observation prove them to have been; and henceforth, by painful

experience, and careful research, and cautious faith, and humble docility, must they gather the fruits of *knowledge*; by a vain desire and false conceit of which, they had forfeited the tree of life. So runs the story

"Of man's first disobedience, and the fruit
Of that forbidden tree, whose mortal taste
Brought death into the world, and all our wo,
With loss of Eden, till one greater Man
Restore us, and regain the blissful seat."

13. The analogy of words in the different languages now known, has been thought by many to be sufficiently frequent and clear to suggest the idea of their common origin. Their differences are indeed great; but perhaps not greater, than the differences in the several races of men, all of whom, as revelation teaches, sprung from one common stock. From the same source we learn, that, till the year of the world 1844, "The whole earth was of one language, and of one speech."—*Gen.*, xi, 1.[22] At that period, the whole world of mankind consisted only of the descendants of the eight souls who had been saved in the ark, and so many of the eight as had survived the flood one hundred and eighty-eight years. Then occurred that remarkable intervention of the Deity, in which he was pleased to confound their language; so that they could not understand one an other's speech, and were consequently scattered abroad upon the face of the earth. This, however, in the opinion of many learned men, does not prove the immediate formation of any new languages.

14. But, whether new languages were thus immediately formed or not, the event, in all probability, laid the foundation for that diversity which subsequently obtained among the languages of the different nations which sprung from the dispersion; and hence it may be regarded as the remote cause of the differences which now exist. But for the immediate origin of

the peculiar characteristical differences which distinguish the various languages now known, we are not able with much certainty to account. Nor is there even much plausibility in the speculations of those grammarians who have attempted to explain the order and manner in which the declensions, the moods, the tenses, or other leading features of the languages, were first introduced. They came into use before they could be generally known, and the partial introduction of them could seldom with propriety be made a subject of instruction or record, even if there were letters and learning at hand to do them this honour. And it is better to be content with ignorance, than to form such conjectures as imply any thing that is absurd or impossible. For instance: Neilson's Theory of the Moods, published in the Classical Journal of 1819, though it exhibits ingenuity and learning, is liable to this strong objection; that it proceeds on the supposition, that the moods of English verbs, and of several other derivative tongues, were invented in a certain order by persons, not speaking a language learned chiefly from their fathers, but uttering a new one as necessity prompted. But when or where, since the building of Babel, has this ever happened? That no dates are given, or places mentioned, the reader regrets, but he cannot marvel.

15. By what successive changes, our words in general, and especially the minor parts of speech, have become what we now find them, and what is their original and proper signification according to their derivation, the etymologist may often show to our entire satisfaction. Every word must have had its particular origin and history; and he who in such things can explain with certainty what is not commonly known, may do some service to science. But even here the utility of his curious inquiries may be overrated; and whenever, for the sake of some favourite theory, he ventures into the regions of conjecture, or allows himself to be seduced from the path of practical instruction, his errors are obstinate, and his guidance is peculiarly deceptive. Men fond of such speculations, and able to support

them with some show of learning, have done more to unsettle the science of grammar, and to divert ingenious teachers from the best methods of instruction, than all other visionaries put together. Etymological inquiries are important, and I do not mean to censure or discourage them, merely as such; but the folly of supposing that in our language words must needs be of the same class, or part of speech, as that to which they may be traced in an other, deserves to be rebuked. The words *the* and *an* may be articles in English, though obviously traceable to something else in Saxon; and a learned man may, in my opinion, be better employed, than in contending that *if, though,* and *although,* are not conjunctions, but verbs!

16. Language is either oral or written; the question of its origin has consequently two parts. Having suggested what seemed necessary respecting the origin of *speech*, I now proceed to that of *writing*. Sheridan says, "We have in use *two kinds of language,* the spoken and the written: the one, the gift of God; the other, the invention of man."—*Elocution*, p. xiv. If this ascription of the two things to their sources, were as just as it is clear and emphatical, both parts of our question would seem to be resolved. But this great rhetorician either forgot his own doctrine, or did not mean what he here says. For he afterwards makes the former kind of language as much a work of art, as any one will suppose the latter to have been. In his sixth lecture, he comments on the gift of speech thus: "But still we are to observe, that nature did no more than furnish the power and means; *she did not give the language,* as in the case of the passions, but left it to the industry of men, to find out and agree upon such articulate sounds, as they should choose to make the symbols of their ideas."—*Ib.*, p. 147. He even goes farther, and supposes certain *tones of the voice* to be things invented by man: "Accordingly, as she did not furnish the *words*, which were to be the symbols of his ideas; neither did she furnish the *tones*, which were to manifest, and communicate by their own virtue, the internal exertions and emotions, of such of his nobler faculties, as chiefly distinguish him from the

brute species; but left them also, like words, to the care and invention of man."—*Ibidem*. On this branch of the subject, enough has already been presented.

17. By most authors, alphabetic writing is not only considered an artificial invention, but supposed to have been wholly unknown in the early ages of the world. Its antiquity, however, is great. Of this art, in which the science of grammar originated, we are not able to trace the commencement. Different nations have claimed the honour of the invention; and it is not decided, among the learned, to whom, or to what country, it belongs. It probably originated in Egypt. For, "The Egyptians," it is said, "paid divine honours to the Inventor of Letters, whom they called *Theuth*: and Socrates, when he speaks of him, considers him as a god, or a god-like man."—*British Gram.*, p. 32. Charles Bucke has it, "That the first inventor of letters is supposed to have been *Memnon*; who was, in consequence, fabled to be the son of Aurora, goddess of the morning."—*Bucke's Classical Gram.*, p. 5. The ancients in general seem to have thought Phoenicia the birthplace of Letters:

> "Phoenicians first, if ancient fame be true,
> The sacred mystery of letters knew;
> They first, by sound, in various lines design'd,
> Express'd the meaning of the thinking mind;
> The power of words by figures rude conveyed,
> And useful science everlasting made."
>   *Rowe's Lucan*, B. iii, l. 334.

18. Some, however, seem willing to think writing coeval with speech. Thus Bicknell, from Martin's Physico-Grammatical Essay: "We are told by Moses, that Adam *gave names to every living creature*;[23] but how those names were written, or what sort of characters he made use of, is not known

to us; nor indeed whether Adam ever made use of a written language at all; since we find no mention made of any in the sacred history."—*Bicknell's Gram.*, Part ii, p. 5. A certain late writer on English grammar, with admirable flippancy, cuts this matter short, as follows,—satisfying himself with pronouncing all speech to be natural, and all writing artificial: "Of how many primary kinds is language? It is of two kinds; natural or spoken, and artificial or written."—*Oliver B. Peirce's Gram.*, p. 15. "Natural language is, to a limited extent, (the representation of the passions,) common to brutes as well as man; but artificial language, being the work of invention, is peculiar to man."—*Ib.*, p. 16.[24]

19. The writings delivered to the Israelites by Moses, are more ancient than any others now known. In the thirty-first chapter of Exodus, it is said, that God "gave unto Moses, upon Mount Sinai, two tables of testimony, tables of stone, *written with the finger of God*." And again, in the thirty-second: "The tables were the work of God, and the writing was *the writing of God*, graven upon the tables." But these divine testimonies, thus miraculously written, do not appear to have been the first writing; for Moses had been previously commanded to write an account of the victory over Amalek, "for a memorial in a book, and rehearse it in the ears of Joshua."—*Exod.*, xvii, 14. This first battle of the Israelites occurred in Rephidim, a place on the east side of the western gulf of the Red Sea, at or near Horeb, but before they came to Sinai, upon the top of which, (on the fiftieth day after their departure from Egypt,) Moses received the ten commandments of the law.

20. Some authors, however, among whom is Dr. Adam Clarke, suppose that in this instance the order of the events is not to be inferred from the order of the record, or that there is room to doubt whether the use of letters was here intended; and that there consequently remains a strong probability, that the sacred Decalogue, which God himself delivered to Moses on Sinai,

A. M. 2513, B. C. 1491, was "the first writing *in alphabetical characters* ever exhibited to the world." See *Clarke's Succession of Sacred Literature*, Vol. i, p. 24. Dr. Scott, in his General Preface to the Bible, seems likewise to favour the same opinion. "Indeed," says he, "there is some probability in the opinion, that the art of writing was first communicated by revelation, to Moses, in order to perpetuate, with certainty, those facts, truths, and laws, which he was employed to deliver to Israel. Learned men find no traces of *literary*, or alphabetical, writing, in the history of the nations, till long after the days of Moses; unless the book of Job may be regarded as an exception. The art of expressing almost an infinite variety of sounds, by the interchanges of a few letters, or marks, seems more like a discovery to man from heaven, than a human invention; and its beneficial effects, and almost absolute necessity, for the preservation and communication of true religion, favour the conjecture."—*Scott's Preface*, p. xiv.

21. The time at which Cadmus, the Phoenician, introduced this art into Greece, cannot be precisely ascertained. There is no reason to believe it was antecedent to the time of Moses; some chronologists make it between two and three centuries later. Nor is it very probable, that Cadmus invented the sixteen letters of which he is said to have made use. His whole story is so wild a fable, that nothing certain can be inferred from it. Searching in vain for his stolen sister—his sister Europa, carried off by Jupiter—he found a wife in the daughter of Venus! Sowing the teeth of a dragon, which had devoured his companions, he saw them spring up to his aid a squadron of armed soldiers! In short, after a series of wonderful achievements and bitter misfortunes, loaded with grief and infirm with age, he prayed the gods to release him from the burden of such a life; and, in pity from above, both he and his beloved Hermíonè were changed into serpents! History, however, has made him generous amends, by ascribing to him the invention of letters, and accounting him the worthy benefactor to whom the world owes all the benefits derived from literature. I would not willingly rob him of this

honour. But I must confess, there is no feature of the story, which I can conceive to give any countenance to his claim; except that as the great progenitor of the race of authors, his sufferings correspond well with the calamities of which that unfortunate generation have always so largely partaken.

22. The benefits of this invention, if it may be considered an invention, are certainly very great. In oral discourse the graces of elegance are more lively and attractive, but well-written books are the grand instructors of mankind, the most enduring monuments of human greatness, and the proudest achievements of human intellect. "The chief glory of a nation," says Dr. Johnson, "arises from its authors." Literature is important, because it is subservient to all objects, even those of the very highest concern. Religion and morality, liberty and government, fame and happiness, are alike interested in the cause of letters. It was a saying of Pope Pius the Second, that, "Common men should esteem learning as silver, noblemen value it as gold, and princes prize it as jewels." The uses of learning are seen in every thing that is not itself useless.[25] It cannot be overrated, but where it is perverted; and whenever that occurs, the remedy is to be sought by opposing learning to learning, till the truth is manifest, and that which is reprehensible, is made to appear so.

23. I have said, learning cannot be overrated, but where it is perverted. But men may differ in their notions of what learning is; and, consequently, of what is, or is not, a perversion of it. And so far as this point may have reference to theology, and the things of God, it would seem that the Spirit of God alone can fully show us its bearings. If the illumination of the Spirit is necessary to an understanding and a reception of scriptural truth, is it not by an inference more erudite than reasonable, that some great men have presumed to limit to a verbal medium the communications of Him who is everywhere His own witness, and who still gives to His own holy oracles

all their peculiar significance and authority? Some seem to think the Almighty has never given to men any notion of Himself, except by words. "Many ideas," says the celebrated Edmund Burke, "have never been at all presented to the senses of any men *but by words,* as God,[26] angels, devils, heaven, and hell, all of which have however a great influence over the passions."—*On the Sublime and [the] Beautiful,* p. 97. That God can never reveal facts or truths except by words, is a position with which I am by no means satisfied. Of the great truths of Christianity, Dr. Wayland, in his Elements of Moral Science, repeatedly avers, "All these being *facts,* can never be known, except *by language,* that is, by revelation."—*First Edition,* p. 132. Again: "All of them being of the *nature of facts,* they could be made known to man *in no other way than by language.*"—*Ib.,* p. 136. But it should be remembered, that these same facts were otherwise made known to the prophets; (1 Pet., i, 11;) and that which has been done, is not impossible, whether there is reason to expect it again or not. So of the Bible, Calvin says, "No man can have the least knowledge of true and sound doctrine, without having been a disciple of the Scripture."—*Institutes,* B. i, Ch. 6. Had Adam, Abel, Enoch, Noah, and Abraham, then, no such knowledge? And if such they had, what Scripture taught them? We ought to value the Scriptures too highly to say of them any thing that is *unscriptural.* I am, however, very far from supposing there is any *other doctrine* which can be safely substituted for the truths revealed of old, the truths contained in the Holy Scriptures of the Old and New Testaments:

"Left only in those written records pure,
Though not but by the Spirit understood." [27]—*Milton.*

CHAPTER V.

OF THE POWER OF LANGUAGE.

"Quis huic studio literarum, quod profitentur ii, qui grammatici vocantur, penitus se dedidit, quin omnem illarum artium pæne infinitam *vim* et *materiam* scientiæ cogitatione comprehenderit?"—CICERO. *De Oratore*, Lib. i, 3.

1. The peculiar *power* of language is another point worthy of particular consideration. The power of an instrument is virtually the power of him who wields it; and, as language is used in common, by the wise and the foolish, the mighty and the impotent, the candid and the crafty, the righteous and the wicked, it may perhaps seem to the reader a difficult matter, to speak intelligibly of its *peculiar power*. I mean, by this phrase, its fitness or efficiency to or for the accomplishment of the purposes for which it is used. As it is the nature of an agent, to be the doer of something, so it is the nature of an instrument, to be that with which something is effected. To make signs, is to do something, and, like all other actions, necessarily implies an agent; so all signs, being things by means of which other things are represented, are obviously the instruments of such representation. Words, then, which represent thoughts, are things in themselves; but, as signs, they are relative to other things, as being the instruments of their communication or preservation. They are relative also to him who utters them, as well as to those who may happen to be instructed or deceived by them. "Was it Mirabeau, Mr. President, or what other master of the human passions, who has told us that words are things? They are indeed things, and things of mighty influence, not only in addresses to the passions and high-wrought feelings of mankind, but in the discussion of legal and political questions also; because a just conclusion is often avoided, or a false one reached, by the adroit substitution of one phrase or one word for an other."—*Daniel Webster, in Congress*, 1833.

2. To speak, is a moral action, the quality of which depends upon the motive, and for which we are strictly accountable. "But I say unto you, that

every idle word that men shall speak, they shall give account thereof in the day of judgement; for by thy words thou shalt be justified, and by thy words thou shalt be condemned."—*Matt.*, xii, 36, 37. To listen, or to refuse to listen, is a moral action also; and there is meaning in the injunction, "Take heed what ye hear."—*Mark*, iv, 24. But why is it, that so much of what is spoken or written, is spoken or written in vain? Is language impotent? It is sometimes employed for purposes with respect to which it is utterly so; and often they that use it, know not how insignificant, absurd, or ill-meaning a thing they make of it. What is said, with whatever inherent force or dignity, has neither power nor value to him who does not understand it;[28] and, as Professor Duncan observes, "No word can be to any man the sign of an idea, till that idea comes to have a real existence in his mind."—*Logic*, p. 62. In instruction, therefore, speech ought not to be regarded as the foundation or the essence of knowledge, but as the sign of it; for knowledge has its origin in the power of sensation, or reflection, or consciousness, and not in that of recording or communicating thought. Dr. Spurzheim was not the first to suggest, "It is time to abandon the immense error of supposing that words and precepts are sufficient to call internal feelings and intellectual faculties into active exercise."—*Spurzheim's Treatise on Education*, p. 94.

3. But to this it may be replied, When God wills, the signs of knowledge are knowledge; and words, when he gives the ability to understand them, may, in some sense, become—"spirit and life." See *John*, vi, 63. Where competent intellectual faculties exist, the intelligible signs of thought do move the mind to think; and to think sometimes with deep feelings too, whether of assent or dissent, of admiration or contempt. So wonderful a thing is a rational soul, that it is hard to say to what ends the language in which it speaks, may, or may not, be sufficient. Let experience determine. We are often unable to excite in others the sentiments which we would: words succeed or fail, as they are received or resisted. But let a scornful

expression be addressed to a passionate man, will not the words "call internal feelings" into action? And how do feelings differ from thoughts? [29] Hear Dr. James Rush: "The human mind is the place of representation of all the existences of nature which are brought within the scope of the senses. The representatives are called ideas. These ideas are the simple passive pictures of things, or [else] they exist with an activity, capable of so affecting the physical organs as to induce us to seek the continuance of that which produces them, or to avoid it. This active or vivid class of ideas comprehends the passions. The functions of the mind here described, exist then in different forms and degrees, from the simple idea, to the highest energy of passion: and the terms, thought, sentiment, emotion, feeling, and passion, are but the verbal signs of these degrees and forms. Nor does there appear to be any line of classification, for separating thought from passion: since simple thoughts, without changing their nature, do, from interest or incitement, often assume the colour of passion."—*Philosophy of the Human Voice*, p. 328.

4. Lord Kames, in the Appendix to his Elements of Criticism, divides *the senses* into external and internal, defining *perception* to be the act by which through the former we know outward objects, and *consciousness* the act by which through the latter we know what is within the mind. An *idea*, according to his definition, (which he says is precise and accurate,) is, "That *perception* of a real object which *is raised* in the mind by the power of *memory*." But among the real objects from which memory may raise ideas, he includes the workings of the mind itself, or whatever we remember of our former passions, emotions, thoughts, or designs. Such a definition, he imagines, might have saved Locke, Berkley, and their followers, from much vain speculation; for with the ideal systems of these philosophers, or with those of Aristotle and Des Cartes, he by no means coincides. This author says, "As ideas are the chief materials employed in reasoning and reflecting, it is of consequence that their nature and differences be

understood. It appears now that ideas may be distinguished into three kinds: first, Ideas derived from original perceptions, properly termed *ideas of memory*; second, Ideas communicated *by language* or other signs; and third, Ideas *of imagination*. These ideas differ from each other in many respects; but chiefly in respect to their *proceeding from different causes*. The first kind is derived from real existences that have been objects of our senses; *language is the cause of the second,* or any other sign that has the same power with language; and a man's imagination is to himself the cause of the third. It is scarce [ly] necessary to add, that an idea, originally of imagination, being conveyed to others by language or any other vehicle, becomes in their mind an idea of the second kind; and again, that an idea of this kind, being afterwards recalled to the mind, becomes in that circumstance an idea of memory."—*El. of Crit.,* Vol. ii, p. 384.

5. Whether, or how far, language is to the mind itself *the instrument of thought,* is a question of great importance in the philosophy of both. Our literature contains occasional assertions bearing upon this point, but I know of no full or able discussion of it.[30] Cardell's instructions proceed upon the supposition, that neither the reason of men, nor even that of superior intelligences, can ever operate independently of words. "Speech," says he, "is to the mind what action is to animal bodies. Its improvement is the improvement of our intellectual nature, and a duty to God who gave it."—*Essay on Language,* p. 3. Again: "An attentive investigation will show, that there is no way in which the individual mind can, within itself, to any extent, *combine its ideas,* but by the intervention of words. Every process of the reasoning powers, beyond the immediate perception of sensible objects, depends on the structure of speech; and, in a great degree, according to the excellence of this *chief instrument of all mental operations,* will be the means of personal improvement, of the social transmission of thought, and the elevation of national character. From this, it may be laid down as a broad principle, that no individual can make great advances in intellectual

improvement, beyond the bounds of a ready-formed language, as the necessary means of his progress."—*Ib.*, p. 9. These positions might easily be offset by contrary speculations of minds of equal rank; but I submit them to the reader, with the single suggestion, that the author is not remarkable for that sobriety of judgement which gives weight to opinions.

6. We have seen, among the citations in a former chapter, that Sanctius says, "Names are the signs, and as it were *the instruments, of things*." But what he meant by "*instrumenta rerum*" is not very apparent. Dr. Adam says, "The principles of grammar may be traced from the progress of the mind in the acquisition of language. Children first express their feelings by motions and gestures of the body, by cries and tears. *This is*[31] the language of nature, and therefore universal. *It fitly represents*[32] the quickness of sentiment and thought, which are as instantaneous as the impression of light on the eye. Hence we always express our stronger feelings by these natural signs. But when we want to make known to others the particular conceptions of the mind, we must represent them by parts, we must divide and analyze them. We express *each part by certain signs*,[33] and join these together, according to the order of their relations. Thus words are *both the instrument and signs*[34] *the division* of thought."—*Preface to Latin Gram.*

7. The utterance of words, or the making of signs of any sort, requires time;[35] but it is here suggested by Dr. Adam, that sentiment and thought, though susceptible of being retained or recalled, naturally flash upon the mind with immeasurable quickness.[36] If so, they must originate in something more spiritual than language. The Doctor does not affirm that words are the instruments of thought, but of *the division* of thought. But it is manifest, that if they effect this, they are not the only instruments by means of which the same thing may be done. The deaf and dumb, though uninstructed and utterly ignorant of language, can think; and can, by rude signs of their own inventing, manifest a similar division, corresponding to the individuality of things. And what else can be meant by "*the division of thought,*" than our notion of objects, as existing severally, or as being distinguishable into parts? There can, I think, be no such division respecting that which is perfectly pure and indivisible in its essence; and, I would ask, is not simple continuity apt to exclude it from our conception of every thing which appears with uniform coherence? Dr. Beattie says, "It appears to me, that, as all things are individuals, all thoughts must be so too."—*Moral Science*, Chap, i, Sec. 1. If, then, our thoughts are thus divided, and consequently, as this author infers, have not in themselves any of that generality which belongs to the signification of common nouns, there is little need of any instrument to divide them further: the mind rather needs help, as Cardell suggests, "to combine its ideas." [37]

8. So far as language is a work of art, and not a thing conferred or imposed upon us by nature, there surely can be in it neither division nor union that was not first in the intellect for the manifestation of which it was formed. First, with respect to generalization. "The human mind," says Harris, "by an energy as spontaneous and familiar to its nature, as the seeing of colour is familiar to the eye, discerns at once what in many is one, what in things dissimilar and different is similar and the same."—*Hermes,* p. 362.

Secondly, with respect to division. Mechanical separations are limited: "But the mind surmounts all power of concretion; and can place in the simplest manner every attribute by itself; convex without concave; colour without superficies; superficies without body; and body without its accidents: as distinctly each one, as though they had never been united. And thus it is, that it penetrates into the recesses of all things, not only dividing them as wholes, into their more conspicuous parts, but persisting till it even separate those elementary principles which, being blended together after a more mysterious manner, are united in the minutest part as much as in the mightiest whole."—*Harris's Hermes*, p. 307.

9. It is remarkable that this philosopher, who had so sublime conceptions of the powers of the human mind, and who has displayed such extraordinary acuteness in his investigations, has represented the formation of words, or the utterance of language, as equalling in speed the progress of our very thoughts; while, as we have seen, an other author, of great name, avers, that thought is "as instantaneous as the impression of light on the eye." Philosophy here too evidently nods. In showing the advantage of words, as compared with pictures, Harris says, "If we consider the ease and speed with which words are formed,-an ease which knows no trouble or fatigue, and a *speed which equals the progress of our very thoughts*,[38]—we may plainly perceive an answer to the question here proposed, Why, in the common intercourse of men with men, imitations have been rejected, and symbols preferred."—*Hermes*, p. 336. Let us hear a third man, of equal note: "Words have been called *winged*; and they well deserve that name, when their abbreviations are compared with the progress which speech could make without these inventions; but, compared with the rapidity of thought, they have not *the smallest claim to that title*. Philosophers have calculated the difference of velocity between sound and light; but who will attempt to calculate the difference between speech and thought!"—*Horne Tooke's Epea Pteroenta*, Vol. i, p. 23.

10. It is certain, that, in the admirable economy of the creation, natures subordinate are made, in a wonderful manner, subservient to the operations of the higher; and that, accordingly, our first ideas are such as are conceived of things external and sensible. Hence all men whose intellect appeals only to external sense, are prone to a philosophy which reverses the order of things pertaining to the mind, and tends to materialism, if not to atheism. "But"—to refer again to Harris—"the intellectual scheme which never forgets Deity, postpones every thing corporeal to the primary mental Cause. It is here it looks for the origin of intelligible ideas, even of those which exist in human capacities. For though sensible objects may be the destined medium to awaken the dormant energies of man's understanding, yet are those energies themselves no more contained, in sense, than the explosion of a cannon, in the spark which gave it fire. In short, all minds that are, are similar and congenial; and so too are their ideas, or intelligible forms. Were it otherwise, there could be no intercourse between man and man, or (what is more important) between man and God."—*Hermes*, p. 393.

11. A doctrine somewhat like this, is found in the Meditations of the emperor Marcus Aurelius Antoninus, though apparently repugnant to the polytheism commonly admitted by the Stoics, to whom he belonged: "The world, take it all together, is but one; there is but one sort of matter to make it of, one God to govern it, and one law to guide it. For, run through the whole system of rational beings, and you will find reason and truth but single and the same. And thus beings of the same kind, and endued with the same reason, are made happy by the same exercises of it."—Book vii, Sec. 9. Again: "Let your soul receive the Deity as your blood does the air; for the influences of the one are no less vital, than those of the other. This correspondence is very practicable: for there is an ambient omnipresent Spirit, which lies as open and pervious to your mind, as the air you breathe does to your lungs: but then you must remember to be disposed to draw it."—Book viii, Sec. 54; *Collier's Translation*.

12. Agreeably to these views, except that he makes a distinction between a natural and a supernatural idea of God, we find Barclay, the early defender of the Quakers, in an argument with a certain Dutch nobleman, philosophizing thus: "If the Scripture then be true, there is in men a supernatural idea of God, which altogether differs from this natural idea—I say, in all men; because all men are capable of salvation, and consequently of enjoying this divine vision. Now this capacity consisteth herein, that they have such a supernatural idea in themselves.[39] For if there were no such idea in them, it were impossible they should so know God; for whatsoever is clearly and distinctly known, is known by its proper idea; neither can it otherwise be clearly and distinctly known. *For the ideas of all things are divinely planted in our souls*; for, as the better philosophy teacheth, they are not begotten in us by outward objects or outward causes, but only are by these outward things excited or stirred up. And this is true, not only in supernatural ideas of God and things divine, and in natural ideas of the natural principles of human understanding, and conclusions thence deduced by the strength of human reason; but even in the ideas of outward objects, which are perceived by the outward senses: as that noble Christian philosopher Boëthius hath well observed; to which also the Cartesian philosophy agreeth." I quote only to show the concurrence of others, with Harris's position. Barclay carries on his argument with much more of a similar import. See *Sewell's History*, folio, p. 620.

13. But the doctrine of ideas existing primarily in God, and being divinely planted in our souls, did not originate with Boëthius: it may be traced back a thousand years from his time, through the philosophy of Proclus, Zeno, Aristotle,[40] Plato, Socrates, Parmenides, and Pythagoras. It is absurd to suppose any production or effect to be more excellent than its cause. That which really produces motion, cannot itself be inert; and that which actually causes the human mind to think and reason, cannot itself be devoid of intelligence. "For knowledge can alone produce knowledge." [41]

A doctrine apparently at variance with this, has recently been taught, with great confidence, among the professed discoveries of *Phrenology*. How much truth there may be in this new "*science*," as it is called, I am not prepared to say; but, as sometimes held forth, it seems to me not only to clash with some of the most important principles of mental philosophy, but to make the power of thought the result of that which is in itself inert and unthinking. Assuming that the primitive faculties of the human understanding have not been known in earlier times, it professes to have discovered, in the physical organization of the brain, their proper source, or essential condition, and the true index to their measure, number, and distribution. In short, the leading phrenologists, by acknowledging no spiritual substance, virtually deny that ancient doctrine, "It is not in flesh to think, or bones to reason," [42] and make the mind either a material substance, or a mere mode without substantial being.

14. "The doctrine of *immaterial substances*," says Dr. Spurzheim, "is not sufficiently amenable to the test of observation; it is founded on belief, and only supported by hypothesis."—*Phrenology*, Vol. i, p. 20. But it should be remembered, that our notion of material substance, is just as much a matter of hypothesis. All accidents, whether they be qualities or actions, we necessarily suppose to have some support; and this we call *substance*, deriving the term from the Latin, or *hypostasis*, if we choose to borrow from the Greek. But what this substance, or hypostasis, is, independently of its qualities or actions, we know not. This is clearly proved by Locke. What do we mean by *matter*? and what by *mind*? *Matter* is that which is solid, extended, divisible, movable, and occupies space. *Mind* is that which thinks, and wills, and reasons, and remembers, and worships. Here are qualities in the one case; operations in the other. Here are two definitions as totally distinct as any two can be; and he that sees not in them a difference of *substance*, sees it nowhere: to him all natures are one; and that one, an absurd supposition.

15. In favour of what is urged by the phrenologists, it may perhaps be admitted, as a natural law, that, "If a picture of a visible object be formed upon the retina, and the impression be communicated, by the nerves, to the brain, the *result* will be an act of perception."—*Wayland's Moral Science*, p. 4. But it does not follow, nor did the writer of this sentence believe, that perception is a mere act or attribute of the organized matter of the brain. A material object can only occasion in our sensible organs a corporeal motion, which has not in it the nature of thought or perception; and upon what principle of causation, shall a man believe, in respect to vision, that the thing which he sees, is more properly the cause of the idea conceived of it, than is the light by which he beholds it, or the mind in which that idea is formed? Lord Kames avers, that, "Colour, which appears to the eye as spread upon a substance, has no existence but in the mind of the spectator."—*Elements of Criticism*, i, 178. And Cicero placed the perception, not only of colour, but of taste, of sound, of smell, and of touch, in the mind, rather than in the senses. "Illud est album, hoc dulce, canorum illud, hoc bene olens, hoc asperum: animo jam hæc tenemus comprehensa, non sensibus."—*Ciceronis Acad.* Lib. ii, 7. Dr. Beattie, however, says: "Colours inhere not in the coloured body, but in the light that falls upon it; * * * and the word *colour* denotes, an external thing, and never a sensation of the mind."—*Moral Science*, i, 54. Here is some difference of opinion; but however the thing may be, it does not affect my argument; which is, that to perceive or think is an act or attribute of our immaterial substance or nature, and not to be supposed the effect either of the objects perceived or of our own corporeal organization.

16. Divine wisdom has established the senses as the avenues through which our minds shall receive notices of the forms and qualities of external things; but the sublime conception of the ancients, that these forms and qualities had an abstract preëxistence in the divine mind, is a common doctrine of many English authors, as Milton, Cowper, Akenside, and others.

For example: "Now if *Ens primum* be the cause of *entia a primo,* then he hath the idea of them in him: for he made them by counsel, and not by necessity; for then he should have needed them, and they have a parhelion of that wisdom that is in his Idea."—*Richardson's Logic*, p. 16: Lond. 1657.

"Then the Great Spirit, whom his works adore,
Within his own deep essence view'd the forms,
The forms eternal of created things."—AKENSIDE.
Pleasures of the Imagination, Book i.

"And in the school of sacred wisdom taught,
To read his wonders, in whose thought the world,
Fair as it is, existed ere it was."—COWPER.
Task: Winter Morning Walk, p. 150.

"Thence to behold this new-created world,
The addition of his empire, how it show'd
In prospect from his throne, how good, how fair,
Answering his great idea."—MILTON.
Paradise Lost, Book vii, line 554.

"Thought shines from God as shines the morn;
Language from kindling thought is born."
ANON.: *a Poem in imitation of Coleridge.*

17. "Original Truth," [43] says Harris, "having the most intimate connection with the *Supreme Intelligence,* may be said (as it were) to shine with unchangeable splendor, enlightening throughout the universe every possible subject, by nature susceptible of its benign influence. Passions and other obstacles may prevent indeed its efficacy, as clouds and vapours may obscure the sun; but itself neither admits diminution, nor change, because the darkness respects only particular percipients. Among *these* therefore we

must look for ignorance and error, and for that *subordination of intelligence* which is their natural consequence. Partial views, the imperfections of sense; inattention, idleness, the turbulence of passions; education, local sentiments, opinions, and belief; conspire in many instances to furnish us with ideas, some too partial, and (what is worse than all this) with many that are erroneous, and contrary to truth. These it behoves us to correct as far as possible, by cool suspense and candid examination. Thus by a connection perhaps little expected, the cause of *Letters*, and that of *Virtue*, appear to coincide; it being the business of both, to examine our ideas, and to amend them by the standard of nature and of truth."—See *Hermes*, p. 406.

18. Although it seems plain from our own consciousness, that the mind is an active self-moving principle or essence, yet capable of being moved, after its own manner, by other causes outward as well as inward; and although it must be obvious to reflection, that all its ideas, perceptions, and emotions, are, with respect to itself, of a spiritual nature—bearing such a relation to the spiritual substance in which alone they appear, as bodily motion is seen to bear to material substances; yet we know, from experience and observation, that they who are acquainted with words, are apt to think in words—that is, mentally to associate their internal conceptions with the verbal signs which they have learned to use. And though I do not conceive the position to be generally true, that words are to the mind itself the necessary instruments of thought, yet, in my apprehension, it cannot well be denied, that in some of its operations and intellectual reaches, the mind is greatly assisted by its own contrivances with respect to language. I refer not now to the communication of knowledge; for, of this, language is admitted to be properly the instrument. But there seem to be some processes of thought, or calculation, in which the mind, by a wonderful artifice in the combination of terms, contrives to prevent embarrassment, and help itself

forward in its conceptions, when the objects before it are in themselves perhaps infinite in number or variety.

19. We have an instance of this in numeration. No idea is more obvious or simple than that of unity, or one. By the continual addition of this, first to itself to make two, and then to each higher combination successively, we form a series of different numbers, which may go on to infinity. In the consideration of these, the mind would not be able to go tar without the help of words, and those peculiarly fitted to the purpose. The understanding would lose itself in the multiplicity, were it not aided by that curious concatenation of names, which has been contrived for the several parts of the succession. As far as *twelve* we make use of simple unrelated terms. Thenceforward we apply derivatives and compounds, formed from these in their regular order, till we arrive at a *hundred*. This one new word, *hundred*, introduced to prevent confusion, has nine hundred and ninety-nine distinct repetitions in connexion with the preceding terms, and thus brings us to a *thousand*. Here the computation begins anew, runs through all the former combinations, and then extends forward, till the word *thousand* has been used nine hundred and ninety-nine thousand times; and then, for ten hundred thousand, we introduce the new word *million*. With this name we begin again as before, and proceed till we have used it a million of times, each combination denoting a number clearly distinguished from every other; and then, in like manner, we begin and proceed, with *billions, trillions, quadrillions, quintillions, etc.*, to any extent we please.

20. Now can any one suppose that words are not here, in some true sense, the instruments of thought, or of the intellectual process thus carried on? Were all these different numbers to be distinguished directly by the mind itself, and denominated by terms destitute of this artificial connexion, it may well be doubted whether the greatest genius in the world would ever be able to do what any child may now effect by this orderly arrangement of

words; that is, to distinguish exactly the several stages of this long progression, and see at a glance how far it is from the beginning of the series. "The great art of knowledge," says Duncan, "lies in managing with skill the capacity of the intellect, and contriving such helps, as, if they strengthen not its natural powers, may yet expose them to no unnecessary fatigue. When ideas become very complex, and by the multiplicity of their parts grow too unwieldy to be dealt with in the lump, we must ease the view of the mind by taking them to pieces, and setting before it the several portions separately, one after an other. By this leisurely survey we are enabled to take in the whole; and if we can draw it into such an orderly combination as will naturally lead the attention, step by step, in any succeeding consideration of the same idea, we shall have it ever at command, and with a single glance of thought be able to run over all its parts."—*Duncan's Logic*, p. 37, Hence we may infer the great importance of method in grammar; the particulars of which, as Quintilian says, are infinite.[44]

21. Words are in themselves but audible or visible signs, mere arbitrary symbols, used, according to common practice and consent, as significant of our ideas or thoughts.[45] But so well are they fitted to be made at will the medium of mental conference, that nothing else can be conceived to equal them for this purpose. Yet it does not follow that they who have the greatest knowledge and command of words, have all they could desire in this respect. For language is in its own nature but an imperfect instrument, and even when tuned with the greatest skill, will often be found inadequate to convey the impression with which the mind may labour. Cicero, that great master of eloquence, frequently confessed, or declared, that words failed him. This, however, may be thought to have been uttered as a mere figure of speech; and some may say, that the imperfection I speak of, is but an incident of the common weakness or ignorance of human nature; and that if a man always knew what to say to an other in order to persuade or confute,

to encourage or terrify him, he would always succeed, and no insufficiency of this kind would ever be felt or imagined. This also is plausible; but is the imperfection less, for being sometimes traceable to an ulterior source? Or is it certain that human languages used by perfect wisdom, would all be perfectly competent to their common purpose? And if some would be found less so than others, may there not be an insufficiency in the very nature of them all?

22. If there is imperfection in any instrument, there is so much the more need of care and skill in the use of it. Duncan, in concluding his chapter about words as signs of our ideas, says, "It is apparent, that we are sufficiently provided with the means' of communicating our thoughts one to another; and that the mistakes so frequently complained of on this head, are wholly owing to ourselves, in not sufficiently defining the terms we use; or perhaps not connecting them with clear and determinate ideas."—*Logic*, p. 69. On the other hand, we find that some of the best and wisest of men confess the inadequacy of language, while they also deplore its misuse. But, whatever may be its inherent defects, or its culpable abuses, it is still to be honoured as almost the only medium for the communication of thought and the diffusion of knowledge. Bishop Butler remarks, in his Analogy of Religion, (a most valuable work, though defective in style,) "So likewise the imperfections attending the only method by which nature enables and directs us to communicate our thoughts to each other, are innumerable. Language is, in its very nature, inadequate, ambiguous, liable to infinite abuse, even from negligence; and so liable to it from design, that every man can deceive and betray by it."—Part ii, Chap. 3. Lord Kames, too, seconds this complaint, at least in part: "Lamentable is the imperfection of language, almost in every particular that falls not under external sense. I am talking of a matter exceedingly clear in the perception, and yet I find no small difficulty to express it clearly in words."—*Elements of Criticism*, Vol. i, p. 86. "All writers," says Sheridan, "seem to be under the influence of one

common delusion, that by the help of words alone, they can communicate all that passes in their minds."—*Lectures on Elocution,* p. xi.

23. Addison also, in apologizing for Milton's frequent use of old words and foreign idioms, says, "I may further add, that Milton's sentiments and ideas were so wonderfully sublime, that it would have been impossible for him to have represented them in their full strength and beauty, without having recourse to these foreign assistances. *Our language sunk under him,* and was unequal to that greatness of soul which furnished him with such glorious conceptions."—*Spectator,* No. 297. This, however, Dr. Johnson seems to regard as a mere compliment to genius; for of Milton he says, "The truth is, that both in prose and verse, he had formed his style by a perverse and pedantick principle." But the grandeur of his thoughts is not denied by the critic; nor is his language censured without qualification. "Whatever be the faults of his diction, he cannot want the praise of copiousness and variety: he was master of his language in its full extent; and has selected the melodious words with such diligence, that from his book alone the Art of English Poetry might be learned."— *Johnson's Life of Milton*: *Lives,* p. 92. 24. As words abstractly considered are empty and vain, being in their nature mere signs, or tokens, which derive all their value from the ideas and feelings which they suggest; it is evident that he who would either speak or write well, must be furnished with something more than a knowledge of sounds and letters. Words fitly spoken are indeed both precious and beautiful—"like apples of gold in pictures of silver." But it is not for him whose soul is dark, whose designs are selfish, whose affections are dead, or whose thoughts are vain, to say with the son of Amram, "My doctrine shall drop as the rain, my speech shall distil as the dew; as the small rain upon the tender herb, and as the showers upon the grass."—*Deut.,* xxxii, 2. It is not for him to exhibit the true excellency of speech, because he cannot feel its power. It is not for him, whatever be the theme, to convince the judgement with deductions of reason, to fire the imagination

with glowing imagery, or win with graceful words the willing ear of taste. His wisdom shall be silence, when men are present; for the soul of manly language, is the soul that thinks and feels as best becomes a man.

CHAPTER VI.

OF THE ORIGIN AND HISTORY OF THE ENGLISH LANGUAGE.

"Non mediocres enim tenebræ in sylva, ubi hæc captanda: neque eon, quo pervenire volumus semitæ tritæ: neque non in tramitibus quædam objecta, quæ euntem retinere possent."—VARRO. *De Lingua Latina,* Lib. iv, p. 4.

1. In order that we may set a just value upon the literary labours of those who, in former times, gave particular attention to the culture of the English language, and that we may the better judge of the credibility of modern pretensions to further improvements, it seems necessary that we should know something of the course of events through which its acknowledged melioration in earlier days took place. For, in this case, the extent of a man's knowledge is the strength of his argument. As Bacon quotes Aristotle, "Qui respiciunt ad pauca, de facili pronunciant." He that takes a narrow view, easily makes up his mind. But what is any opinion worth, if further knowledge of facts can confute it?

2. Whatsoever is successively varied, or has such a manner of existence as time can affect, must have had both an origin and a progress; and may have also its particular *history,* if the opportunity for writing it be not neglected. But such is the levity of mankind, that things of great moment are often left without memorial, while the hand of Literature is busy to beguile the world with trifles or with fictions, with fancies or with lies. The

rude and cursory languages of barbarous nations, till the genius of Grammar arise to their rescue, are among those transitory things which unsparing time is ever hurrying away, irrecoverably, to oblivion. Tradition knows not what they were; for of their changes she takes no account. Philosophy tells us, they are resolved into the variable, fleeting breath of the successive generations of those by whom they were spoken; whose kindred fate it was, to pass away unnoticed and nameless, lost in the elements from which they sprung.

3. Upon the history of the English language, darkness thickens as we tread back the course of time. The subject of our inquiry becomes, at every step, more difficult and less worthy. We have now a tract of English literature, both extensive and luminous; and though many modern writers, and no few even of our writers on grammar, are comparatively very deficient in style, it is safe to affirm that the English language in general has never been written or spoken with more propriety and elegance, than it is at the present day. Modern English we read with facility; and that which was good two centuries ago, though considerably antiquated, is still easily understood. The best way, therefore, to gain a practical knowledge of the changes which our language has undergone, is, to read some of our older authors in retrograde order, till the style employed at times more and more remote, becomes in some degree familiar. Pursued in this manner, the study will be less difficult, and the labour of the curious inquirer, which may be suspended or resumed at pleasure, will be better repaid, than if he proceed in the order of history, and attempt at first the Saxon remains.

4. The value of a language as an object of study, depends chiefly on the character of the *books* which it contains; and, secondarily, on its connexion with others more worthy to be thoroughly known. In this instance, there are several circumstances which are calculated soon to discourage research. As our language took its rise during the barbarism of the dark ages, the books

through which its early history must be traced, are not only few and meagre, but, in respect to grammar, unsettled and diverse. It is not to be expected that inquiries of this kind will ever engage the attention of any very considerable number of persons. Over the minds of the reading public, the attractions of novelty hold a much greater influence, than any thing that is to be discovered in the dusk of antiquity. All old books contain a greater or less number of obsolete words, and antiquated modes of expression, which puzzle the reader, and call him too frequently to his glossary. And even the most common terms, when they appear in their ancient, unsettled orthography, are often so disguised as not to be readily recognized.

5. These circumstances (the last of which should be a caution to us against innovations in spelling) retard the progress of the reader, impose a labour too great for the ardour of his curiosity, and soon dispose him to rest satisfied with an ignorance, which, being general, is not likely to expose him to censure. For these reasons, ancient authors are little read; and the real antiquary is considered a man of odd habits, who, by a singular propensity, is led into studies both unfashionable and fruitless—a man who ought to have been born in the days of old, that he might have spoken the language he is so curious to know, and have appeared in the costume of an age better suited to his taste.

6. But *Learning* is ever curious to explore the records of time, as well as the regions of space; and wherever her institutions flourish, she will amass her treasures, and spread them before her votaries. Difference of languages she easily overcomes; but the leaden reign of unlettered Ignorance defies her scrutiny. Hence, of one period of the world's history, she ever speaks with horror—that "long night of apostasy," during which, like a lone Sibyl, she hid her precious relics in solitary cells, and fleeing from degraded Christendom, sought refuge with the eastern caliphs. "This awful decline of true religion in the world carried with it almost every vestige of civil liberty,

of classical literature, and of scientific knowledge; and it will generally be found in experience that they must all stand or fall together."—*Hints on Toleration*, p. 263. In the tenth century, beyond which we find nothing that bears much resemblance to the English language as now written, this mental darkness appears to have gathered to its deepest obscuration; and, at that period, England was sunk as low in ignorance, superstition, and depravity, as any other part of Europe.

7. The English language gradually varies as we trace it back, and becomes at length identified with the Anglo-Saxon; that is, with the dialect spoken by the Saxons after their settlement in England. These Saxons were a fierce, warlike, unlettered people from Germany; whom the ancient Britons had invited to their assistance against the Picts and Scots. Cruel and ignorant, like their Gothic kindred, who had but lately overrun the Roman empire, they came, not for the good of others, but to accommodate themselves. They accordingly seized the country; destroyed or enslaved the ancient inhabitants; or, more probably, drove the remnant of them into the mountains of Wales. Of Welsh or ancient British words, Charles Bucke, who says in his grammar that he took great pains to be accurate in his scale of derivation, enumerates but one hundred and eleven, as now found in our language; and Dr. Johnson, who makes them but ninety-five, argues from their paucity, or almost total absence, that the Saxons could not have mingled at all with these people, or even have retained them in vassalage.

8. The ancient languages of France and of the British isles are said to have proceeded from an other language yet more ancient, called the *Celtic*; so that, from one common source, are supposed to have sprung the present Welsh, the present Irish, and the present Highland Scotch.[46] The term *Celtic* Dr. Webster defines, as a noun, "The language of the Celts;" and, as an adjective, "Pertaining to the primitive inhabitants of the south and west of Europe, or to the early inhabitants of Italy, Gaul, Spain, and Britain."

What *unity*, according to this, there was, or could have been, in the ancient Celtic tongue, does not appear from books, nor is it easy to be conjectured. [47] Many ancient writers sustain this broad application of the term *Celtæ* or *Celts*; which, according to Strabo's etymology of it, means horsemen, and seems to have been almost as general as our word *Indians*. But Cæsar informs us that the name was more particularly claimed by the people who, in his day, lived in France between the Seine and the Garonne, and who by the Romans were called *Galli,* or *Gauls*.

9. The *Celtic* tribes are said to have been the descendants of Gomer, the son of Japhet. The English historians agree that the first inhabitants of their island owed their origin and their language to the *Celtæ*, or Gauls, who settled on the opposite shore. Julius Cæsar, who invaded Britain about half a century before the Christian era, found the inhabitants ignorant of letters, and destitute of any history but oral tradition. To this, however, they paid great attention, teaching every thing in verse. Some of the Druids, it is said in Cæsar's Commentaries, spent twenty years in learning to repeat songs and hymns that were never committed to writing. These ancient priests, or diviners, are represented as having great power, and as exercising it in some respects beneficially; but their horrid rites, with human sacrifices, provoked the Romans to destroy them. Smollett says, "Tiberius suppressed those human sacrifices in Gaul; and Claudius destroyed the Druids of that country; but they subsisted in Britain till the reign of Nero, when Paulus Suetonius reduced the island of Anglesey, which was the place of their retreat, and overwhelmed them with such unexpected and sudden destruction, that all their knowledge and tradition, conveyed to them in the songs of their predecessors, perished at once."—*Smollett's Hist. of Eng.,* 4to, B. i, Ch. i, §7.

10. The Romans considered Britain a province of their empire, for a period of about five hundred years; but the northern part of the island was

never entirely subdued by them, and not till Anno Domini 78, a hundred and thirty-three years after their first invasion of the country, had they completed their conquest of England. Letters and arts, so far at least as these are necessary to the purposes of war or government, the victors carried with them; and under their auspices some knowledge of Christianity was, at a very early period, introduced into Britain. But it seems strange, that after all that is related of their conquests, settlements, cities, fortifications, buildings, seminaries, churches, laws, &c., they should at last have left the Britons in so helpless, degraded, and forlorn a condition. They *did not sow among them the seeds* of any permanent improvement.

11. The Roman government, being unable to sustain itself at home, withdrew its forces finally from Britain in the year 446, leaving the wretched inhabitants almost as savage as it found them, and in a situation even less desirable. Deprived of their native resources, their ancient independence of spirit, as well as of the laws, customs, institutions, and leaders, that had kept them together under their old dynasties, and now deserted by their foreign protectors, they were apparently left at the mercy of blind fortune, the wretched vicissitudes of which there was none to foresee, none to resist. The glory of the Romans now passed away. The mighty fabric of their own proud empire crumbled into ruins. Civil liberty gave place to barbarism; Christian truth, to papal superstition; and the lights of science were put out by both. The shades of night gathered over all; settling and condensing, "till almost every point of that wide horizon, over which the Sun of Righteousness had diffused his cheering rays, was enveloped in a darkness more awful and more portentous than that which of old descended upon rebellious Pharaoh and the callous sons of Ham."—*Hints on Toleration*, p. 310.

12. The Saxons entered Britain in the year 449. But what was the form of their language at that time, cannot now be known. It was a dialect of the

Gothic or *Teutonic*; which is considered the parent of all the northern tongues of Europe, except some few of Sclavonian origin. The only remaining monument of the Gothic language is a copy of the Gospels, translated by Ulphilas; which is preserved at Upsal, and called, from its embellishments, *the Silver Book*. This old work has been three times printed in England. We possess not yet in America all the advantages which may be enjoyed by literary men in the land of our ancestors; but the stores of literature, both ancient and modern, are somewhat more familiar to us, than is there supposed; and the art of printing is fast equalizing, to all nations that cultivate learning, the privilege of drinking at its ancient fountains.

13. It is neither liberal nor just to argue unfavourably of the intellectual or the moral condition of any remote age or country, merely from our own ignorance of it. It is true, we can derive from no quarter a favourable opinion of the state of England after the Saxon invasion, and during the tumultuous and bloody government of the heptarchy. But I will not darken the picture through design. If justice were done to the few names—to Gildas the wise, the memorialist of his country's sufferings and censor of the nation's depravity, who appears a solitary star in the night of the sixth century—to the venerable Bede, the greatest theologian, best scholar, and only historian of the seventh—to Alcuin, the abbot of Canterbury, the luminary of the eighth—to Alfred the great, the glory of the ninth, great as a prince, and greater as a scholar, seen in the evening twilight of an age in which the clergy could not read;—if justice were done to all such, we might find something, even in these dark and rugged times, if not to soften the grimness of the portrait, at least to give greater distinctness of feature.

14. In tracing the history of our language, Dr. Johnson, who does little more than give examples, cites as his first specimen of ancient English, a portion of king [sic—KTH] Alfred's paraphrase in imitation of Boëthius. But this language of Alfred's is not English; but rather, as the learned doctor

himself considered it, an example of the Anglo-Saxon in its highest state of purity. This dialect was first changed by admixture with words derived from the Danish and the Norman; and, still being comparatively rude and meagre, afterwards received large accessions from the Latin, the French, the Greek, the Dutch—till, by gradual changes, which the etymologist may exhibit, there was at length produced a language bearing a sufficient resemblance to the present English, to deserve to be called English at this day.

15. The formation of our language cannot with propriety be dated earlier than the thirteenth century. It was then that a free and voluntary amalgamation of its chief constituent materials took place; and this was somewhat earlier than we date the revival of learning. The English of the thirteenth century is scarcely intelligible to the modern reader. Dr. Johnson calls it "a kind of intermediate diction, neither Saxon nor English;" and says, that Sir John Gower, who wrote in the latter part of the fourteenth century, was "the first of our authors who can be properly said to have written English." Contemporary with Gower, the father of English poetry, was the still greater poet, his disciple Chaucer; who embraced many of the tenets of Wickliffe, and imbibed something of the spirit of the reformation, which was now begun.

16. The literary history of the fourteenth and fifteenth centuries is full of interest; for it is delightful to trace the progress of great and obvious improvement. The reformation of religion and the revival of learning were nearly simultaneous. Yet individuals may have acted a conspicuous part in the latter, who had little to do with the former; for great learning does not necessarily imply great piety, though, as Dr. Johnson observes, "the Christian religion always implies or produces a certain degree of civility and learning."—*Hist. Eng. Lang. before his 4to Dict.* "The ordinary instructions of the clergy, both philosophical and religious, gradually fell

into contempt, as the Classics superseded the one, and the Holy Scriptures expelled the other. The first of these changes was effected by *the early grammarians* of Europe; and it gave considerable aid to the reformation, though it had no immediate connexion with that event. The revival of the English Bible, however, completed the work: and though its appearance was late, and its progress was retarded in every possible manner, yet its dispersion was at length equally rapid, extensive, and effectual."—*Constable's Miscellany*, Vol. xx, p. 75.

17. Peculiar honour is due to those who lead the way in whatever advances human happiness. And, surely, our just admiration of the character of the *reformers* must be not a little enhanced, when we consider what they did for letters as well as for the church. Learning does not consist in useless jargon, in a multitude of mere words, or in acute speculations remote from practice; else the seventeen folios of St. Thomas Aquinas, the angelical doctor of the thirteenth century, and the profound disputations of his great rival, Duns Scotus the subtle, for which they were revered in their own age, had not gained them the contempt of all posterity. From such learning the lucid reasoning of the reformers delivered the halls of instruction. The school divinity of the middle ages passed away before the presence of that which these men learned from the Bible, as did in a later age the Aristotelian philosophy before that which Bacon drew from nature.

18. Towards the latter part of the fourteenth century, Wickliffe furnished the first entire translation of the Bible into English. In like manner did the Germans, a hundred and fifty years after, receive it in their tongue from the hands of Luther; who says, that at twenty years of age, he himself had not seen it in any language. Wickliffe's English style is elegant for the age in which he lived, yet very different from what is elegant now. This first English translation of the Bible, being made about a hundred years before the introduction of printing into England, could not have been very

extensively circulated. A large specimen of it may be seen in Dr. Johnson's History of the English Language. Wickliffe died in 1384. The art of printing was invented about 1440, and first introduced into England, in 1468; but the first printed edition of the Bible in English, was executed in Germany. It was completed, October 5th, 1535.

19. "Martin Luther, about the year 1517, first introduced metrical psalmody into the service of the church, which not only kept alive the enthusiasm of the reformers, but formed a rallying point for his followers. This practice spread in all directions; and it was not long ere six thousand persons were heard singing together at St. Paul's Cross in London. Luther was a poet and musician; but the same talent existed not in his followers. Thirty years afterwards, Sternhold versified fifty-one of the Psalms; and in 1562, with the help of Hopkins, he completed the Psalter. These poetical effusions were chiefly sung to German melodies, which the good taste of Luther supplied: but the Puritans, in a subsequent age, nearly destroyed these germs of melody, assigning as a reason, that music should be so simplified as to suit all persons, and that all may join."—*Dr. Gardiner's Music of Nature*, p. 283.

20. "The schools and colleges of England in the fifteenth and sixteenth centuries were not governed by a system of education which would render their students very eminent either as scholars or as gentlemen: and the monasteries, which were used as seminaries, even until the reformation, taught only the corrupt Latin used by the ecclesiastics. The time however was approaching, when the united efforts of Stanbridge, Linacre, Sir John Cheke, Dean Colet, Erasmus, William Lily, Roger Ascham, &c., were successful in reviving the Latin tongue in all its purity; and even in exciting a taste for Greek in a nation the clergy of which opposed its introduction with the same vehemence which characterized their enmity to a reformation in religion. The very learned Erasmus, the first who undertook the teaching

of the Greek language at Oxford, met with few friends to support him; notwithstanding Oxford was the seat of nearly all the learning in England."—*Constable's Miscellany*, Vol. xx, p. 146.

21. "The priests preached against it, as a very recent invention of the arch-enemy; and confounding in their misguided zeal, the very foundation of their faith, with the object of their resentment, they represented the New Testament itself as 'an impious and dangerous book,' because it was written in that heretical language. Even after the accession of Henry VIII, when Erasmus, who had quitted Oxford in disgust, returned under his especial patronage, with the support of several eminent scholars and powerful persons, his progress was still impeded, and the language opposed. The University was divided into parties, called Greeks and Trojans, the latter being the strongest, from being favoured by the monks; and the Greeks were driven from the streets, with hisses and other expressions of contempt. It was not therefore until Henry VIII and Cardinal Wolsey gave it their positive and powerful protection, that this persecuted language was allowed to be quietly studied, even in the institutions dedicated to learning."—*Ib.*, p. 147.

22. These curious extracts are adduced to show the *spirit of the times*, and the obstacles then to be surmounted in the cause of learning. This popular opposition to Greek, did not spring from a patriotic design to prefer and encourage English literature; for the improvement of this was still later, and the great promoters of it were all of them classical scholars. They wrote in English, not because they preferred it, but because none but those who were bred in colleges, could read any thing else; and, even to this very day, the grammatical study of the English language is shamefully neglected in what are called the higher institutions of learning. In alleging this neglect, I speak comparatively. Every student, on entering upon the practical business of life, will find it of far more importance to him, to be skillful in the language

of his own country than to be distinguished for any knowledge which the learned only can appreciate. "Will the greatest Mastership in Greek and Latin, or [the] translating [of] these Languages into English, avail for the Purpose of acquiring an elegant English Style? No—we know just the Reverse from woeful Experience! And, as Mr. Locke and the Spectator observe, Men who have threshed hard at Greek and Latin for ten or eleven years together, are very often deficient in their own Language."—*Preface to the British Gram.*, 8vo, 1784, p. xxi.

23. That the progress of English literature in early times was slow, will not seem wonderful to those who consider what is affirmed of the progress of other arts, more immediately connected with the comforts of life. "Down to the reign of Elizabeth, the greater part of the houses in considerable towns, had no chimneys: the fire was kindled against the wall, and the smoke found its way out as well as it could, by the roof, the door, or the windows. The houses were mostly built of wattling, plastered over with clay; and the beds were only straw pallets, with a log of wood for a pillow. In this respect, even the king fared no better than his subjects; for, in Henry the Eighth's time, we find directions, 'to examine every night the straw of the king's bed, that no daggers might be concealed therein.' A writer in 1577, speaking of the progress of luxury, mentions three things especially, that were 'marvellously altered for the worse in England;' the multitude of chimneys lately erected, the increase of lodgings, and the exchange of treen platters into pewter, and wooden spoons into silver and tin; and he complains bitterly that oak instead of willow was employed in the building of houses."—REV. ROYAL ROBBINS: *Outlines of History*, p. 377.

24. Shakspeare appeared in the reign of Elizabeth; outlived her thirteen years; and died in 1616 aged 52. The English language in his hands did not lack power or compass of expression. His writings are now more extensively read, than any others of that age; nor has any very considerable

part of his phraseology yet become obsolete. But it ought to be known, that the printers or editors of the editions which are now read, have taken extensive liberty in modernizing his orthography, as well as that of other old authors still popular. How far such liberty is justifiable, it is difficult to say. Modern readers doubtless find a convenience in it. It is very desirable that the orthography of our language should be made uniform, and remain permanent. Great alterations cannot be suddenly introduced; and there is, in stability, an advantage which will counterbalance that of a slow approximation to regularity. Analogy may sometimes decide the form of variable words, but the concurrent usage of the learned must ever be respected, in this, as in every other part of grammar.

25. Among the earliest of the English grammarians, was Ben Jonson, the poet; who died in the year 1637, at the age of sixty-three. His grammar, (which Horne Tooke mistakingly calls "the *first* as well as the *best* English grammar,") is still extant, being published in the several editions of his works. It is a small treatise, and worthy of attention only as a matter of curiosity. It is written in prose, and designed chiefly for the aid of foreigners. Grammar is an unpoetical subject, and therefore not wisely treated, as it once very generally was, in verse. But every poet should be familiar with the art, because the formal principles of his own have always been considered as embraced in it. To its poets, too, every language must needs be particularly indebted; because their compositions, being in general more highly finished than works in prose, are supposed to present the language in its most agreeable form. In the preface to the Poems of Edmund Waller, published in 1690, the editor ventures to say, "He was, indeed, the Parent of English Verse, and the first that shewed us our Tongue had Beauty and Numbers in it. Our Language owes more to Him, than the French does to Cardinal Richelieu and the whole Academy. * * * * The Tongue came into His hands a rough diamond: he polished it first; and to *that* degree, that

all artists since him have admired the workmanship, without pretending to mend it."—*British Poets*, Vol. ii, Lond., 1800: *Waller's Poems*, p. 4.

26. Dr. Johnson, however, in his Lives of the Poets, abates this praise, that he may transfer the greater part of it to Dryden and Pope. He admits that, "After about half a century of forced thoughts and rugged metre, some advances towards nature and harmony had been already made by Waller and Denham;" but, in distributing the praise of this improvement, he adds, "It may be doubted whether Waller and Denham could have over-born [*overborne*] the prejudices which had long prevailed, and which even then were sheltered by the protection of Cowley. The new versification, as it was called, may be considered as owing its establishment to Dryden; from whose time it is apparent that English poetry has had no tendency to relapse to its former savageness."—*Johnson's Life of Dryden: Lives*, p. 206. To Pope, as the translator of Homer, he gives this praise: "His version may be said to have tuned the English tongue; for since its appearance no writer, however deficient in other powers, has wanted melody."—*Life of Pope: Lives*, p. 567. Such was the opinion of Johnson; but there are other critics who object to the versification of Pope, that it is "monotonous and cloying." See, in Leigh Hunt's Feast of the Poets, the following couplet, and a note upon it:

"But ever since Pope spoil'd the ears of the town
With his cuckoo-song verses half up and half down."

27. The unfortunate Charles I, as well as his father James I, was a lover and promoter of letters. He was himself a good scholar, and wrote well in English, for his time: he ascended the throne in 1625, and was beheaded in 1648. Nor was Cromwell himself, with all his religious and military enthusiasm, wholly insensible to *literary* merit. This century was distinguished by the writings of Milton, Dryden, Waller, Cowley, Denham,

Locke, and others; and the reign of Charles II, which is embraced in it, has been considered by some "the Augustan age of English literature." But that honour, if it may well be bestowed on any, belongs rather to a later period. The best works produced in the eighteenth century, are so generally known and so highly esteemed, that it would be lavish of the narrow space allowed to this introduction, to speak particularly of their merits. Some grammatical errors may be found in almost all books; but our language was, in general, written with great purity and propriety by Addison, Swift, Pope, Johnson, Lowth, Hume, Horne, and many other celebrated authors who flourished in the last century. Nor was it much before this period, that the British writers took any great pains to be accurate in the use of their own language;

"Late, very late, correctness grew our care,
When the tir'd nation breath'd from civil war."—*Pope*.

28. English books began to be printed in the early part of the sixteenth century; and, as soon as a taste for reading was formed, the press threw open the flood-gates of general knowledge, the streams of which are now pouring forth, in a copious, increasing, but too often turbid tide, upon all the civilized nations of the earth. This mighty engine afforded a means by which superior minds could act more efficiently and more extensively upon society in general. And thus, by the exertions of genius adorned with learning, our native tongue has been made the polished vehicle of the most interesting truths, and of the most important discoveries; and has become a language copious, strong, refined, and capable of no inconsiderable degree of harmony. Nay, it is esteemed by some who claim to be competent judges, to be the strongest, the richest, the most elegant, and the most susceptible of sublime imagery, of all the languages in the world.

CHAPTER VII.

CHANGES AND SPECIMENS OF THE ENGLISH LANGUAGE.

"Quot enim verba, et nonnunquam in deterius, hoc, quo vivimus, sæculo, partim aliqâ, partim nullâ necessitate cogente, mutata sunt?"—ROB. AINSWORTH: *Lat. Dict., 4to*; Præf., p. xi.

1. In the use of language, every one chooses his words from that common stock which he has learned, and applies them in practice according to his own habits and notions. If the style of different writers of the same age is various, much greater is the variety which appears in the productions of different ages. Hence the date of a book may often be very plausibly conjectured from the peculiarities of its style. As to what is best in itself, or best adapted to the subject in hand, every writer must endeavour to become his own judge. He who, in any sort of composition, would write with a master's hand, must first apply himself to books with a scholar's diligence. He must think it worth his while to inform himself, that he may be critical. Desiring to give the student all the advantage, entertainment, and satisfaction, that can be expected from a work of this kind, I shall subjoin a few brief specimens in illustration of what has been said in the foregoing chapter. The order of time will be followed *inversely*; and, as Saxon characters are not very easily obtained, or very apt to be read, the Roman letters will be employed for the few examples to which the others would be more appropriate. But there are some peculiarities of ancient usage in English, which, for the information of the young reader, it is proper in the first place to explain.

2. With respect to the letters, there are *several changes* to be mentioned. (1.) The pages of old books are often crowded with capitals: it was at one time the custom to distinguish all nouns, and frequently verbs, or any other important words, by heading them with a great letter. (2.) The letter Ess, of the lower case, had till lately two forms, the long and the short, as [tall-s]

and s; the former very nearly resembling the small f, and the latter, its own capital. The short *s* was used *at the end of words*, and the long *[tall-s]*, in other places; but the latter is now laid aside, in favour of the more distinctive form. (3.) The letters *I* and *J* were formerly considered as one and the same. Hence we find *hallelujah* for *halleluiah*, *Iohn* for *John*, *iudgement* for *judgement*, &c. And in many dictionaries, the words beginning with *J* are still mixed with those which begin with *I*. (4.) The letters *U* and *V* were mixed in like manner, and for the same reason; the latter being a consonant power given to the former, and at length distinguished from it by a different form. Or rather, the figure of the capital seems to have been at last appropriated to the one, and that of the small letter to the other. But in old books the forms of these two letters are continually confounded or transposed. Hence it is, that our *Double-u* is composed of two *Vees*; which, as we see in old books, were sometimes printed separately: as, VV, for W; or vv, for w.

3. The *orthography* of our language, rude and unsettled as it still is in many respects, was formerly much more variable and diverse. In books a hundred years old or more, we often find the most common words spelled variously by the same writer, and even upon the very same page. With respect to the forms of words, a few particulars may here be noticed: (1.) The article *an*, from which the *n* was dropped before words beginning with a consonant sound, is often found in old books where *a* would be more proper; as, *an heart, an help, an hill, an one, an use*. (2.) Till the seventeenth century, the possessive case was written without the apostrophe; being formed at different times, in *es, is, ys, or s*, like the plural; and apparently without rule or uniformity in respect to the doubling of the final consonant: as *Goddes, Godes, Godis, Godys*, or *Gods*, for *God's*; so *mannes, mannis, mannys* or *mans*, for *man's*. Dr. Ash, whose English Grammar was in some repute in the latter part of the eighteenth century, argued against the use of the apostrophe, alleging that it was

seldom used to distinguish the possessive case till about the beginning of that century; and he then prophesied that the time would come, when *correct writers would lay it aside again*, as a strange corruption, an improper "departure from the original formation" of that case of English nouns. And, among the speculations of these latter days, I have somewhere seen an attempt to disparage this useful sign, and explode it, as an unsightly thing *never well established*. It does not indeed, like a syllabic sign, inform the ear or affect the sound; but still it is useful, because it distinguishes to the eye, not only the *case*, but the *number*, of the nouns thus marked. Pronouns, being different in their declension, do not need it, and should therefore always be written without it.

4. The common usage of those who have spoken English, has always inclined rather to brevity than to melody; contraction and elision of the ancient terminations of words, constitute no small part of the change which has taken place, or of the difference which perhaps always existed between the solemn and the familiar style. In respect to euphony, however, these terminations have certainly nothing to boast; nor does the earliest period of the language appear to be that in which they were the most generally used without contraction. That degree of smoothness of which the tongue was anciently susceptible, had certainly no alliance with these additional syllables. The long sonorous endings which constitute the declensions and conjugations of the most admired languages, and which seem to chime so well with the sublimity of the Greek, the majesty of the Latin, the sweetness of the Italian, the dignity of the Spanish, or the polish of the French, *never had* any place in English. The inflections given to our words never embraced any other vowel power than that of the short *e* or *i*; and even, this we are inclined to dispense with, whenever we can; so that most of our grammatical inflections are, to the ear, nothing but consonants blended with the final syllables of the words to which they are added. *Ing* for the first participle, *er* for the comparative degree, and *est* for the superlative, are

indeed added as whole syllables; but the rest, as *d* or *ed* for preterits and perfect participles, *s* or *es* for the plural number of nouns, or for the third person singular of verbs, and *st* or *est* for the second person singular of verbs, nine times in ten, fall into the sound or syllable with which the primitive word terminates. English verbs, as they are now commonly used, run through their entire conjugation without acquiring a single syllable from inflection, except sometimes when the sound of *d, s,* or *st* cannot be added to them.

5. This simplicity, so characteristic of our modern English, as well as of the Saxon tongue, its proper parent, is attended with advantages that go far to compensate for all that is consequently lost in euphony, or in the liberty of transposition. Our formation of the moods and tenses, by means of a few separate auxiliaries, all monosyllabic, and mostly without inflection, is not only simple and easy, but beautiful, chaste, and strong. In my opinion, our grammarians have shown far more affection for the obsolete or obsolescent terminations *en, eth, est,* and *edst,* than they really deserve. Till the beginning of the sixteenth century, *en* was used to mark the plural number of verbs, as, *they sayen* for *they say*; after which, it appears to have been dropped. Before the beginning of the seventeenth century, *s* or *es* began to dispute with *th* or *eth* the right of forming the third person singular of verbs; and, as the Bible and other grave books used only the latter, a clear distinction obtained, between the solemn and the familiar style, which distinction is well known at this day. Thus we have, *He runs, walks, rides, reaches*, &c., for the one; and, *He runneth, walketh, rideth, reacheth*, &c., for the other. About the same time, or perhaps earlier, the use of the second person singular began to be avoided in polite conversation, by the substitution of the plural verb and pronoun; and, when used in poetry, it was often contracted, so as to prevent any syllabic increase. In old books, all verbs and participles that were intended to be contracted in pronunciation, were contracted also, in some way, by the writer: as, "*call'd, carry'd,*

sacrific'd;" "fly'st, ascrib'st, cryd'st;" "tost, curst, blest, finisht;" and others innumerable. All these, and such as are like them, we now pronounce in the same way, but usually write differently; as, *called, carried, sacrificed; fliest, ascribest, criettst; tossed, cursed, blessed, finished.* Most of these topics will be further noticed in the Grammar.

I. ENGLISH OF THE NINETEENTH CENTURY.

6. *Queen Victoria's Answer to an Address.—Example written in 1837.*

"I thank you for your condolence upon the death of his late Majesty, for the justice which you render to his character, and to the measures of his reign, and for your warm congratulations upon my accession to the throne. I join in your prayers for the prosperity of my reign, the best security for which is to be found in reverence for our holy religion, and in the observance of its duties."—VICTORIA, *to the Friends' Society.*

7. *From President Adams's Eulogy on Lafayette.—Written in 1834.*

"Pronounce him one of the first men of his age, and you have yet not done him justice. Try him by that test to which he sought in vain to stimulate the vulgar and selfish spirit of Napoleon; class him among the men who, to compare and seat themselves, must take in the compass of all ages; turn back your eyes upon the records of time; summon from the creation of the world to this day the mighty dead of every age and every clime; and where, among the race of merely mortal men, shall one be found, who, as the benefactor of his kind, shall claim to take precedence of Lafayette?"—JOHN QUINCY ADAMS.

8. *From President Jackson's Proclamation against Nullification.—1832.*

"No, we have not erred! The Constitution is still the object of our reverence, the bond of our Union, our defence in danger, the source of our prosperity in peace. It shall descend, as we have received it, uncorrupted by sophistical construction, to our posterity: and the sacrifices of local interest, of State prejudices, of personal animosities, that were made to bring it into existence, will again be patriotically offered for its support."—ANDREW JACKSON.

9. *From a Note on one of Robert Hall's Sermons.—Written about 1831.*

"After he had written down the striking apostrophe which occurs at about page 76 of most of the editions—'Eternal God! on what are thine enemies intent! what are those enterprises of guilt and horror, that, for the safety of their performers, require to be enveloped in a darkness which the eye of Heaven must not *penetrate*!'—he asked, 'Did I say *penetrate*, sir, when I preached, it?' 'Yes.' 'Do you think, sir, I may venture to alter it? for no man who considered the force of the English language, would use a word of three syllables there, but from absolute necessity.' 'You are doubtless at liberty to alter it, if you think well.' 'Then be so good, sir, as to take your pencil, and for *penetrate* put *pierce*; *pierce* is the word, sir, and the only word to be used there.'"—OLINTHUS GREGORY.

10. *King William's Answer to an Address.—Example written in 1830.*

"I thank you sincerely for your condolence with me, on account of the loss which I have sustained, in common with my people, by the death of my lamented brother, his late Majesty. The assurances which you have conveyed to me, of loyalty and affectionate attachment to my person, are very gratifying to my feelings. You may rely upon my favour and protection, and upon my anxious endeavours to promote morality and true piety among all classes of my subjects."—WILLIAM IV, *to the Friends*.

11. *Reign of George IV, 1830 back to 1820.—Example written in 1827.*

"That morning, thou, that slumbered[48] not before,
Nor slept, great Ocean I laid thy waves to rest,
And hushed thy mighty minstrelsy. No breath
Thy deep composure stirred, no fin, no oar;
Like beauty newly dead, so calm, so still,
So lovely, thou, beneath the light that fell
From angel-chariots sentinelled on high,
Reposed, and listened, and saw thy living change,
Thy dead arise. Charybdis listened, and Scylla;
And savage Euxine on the Thracian beach
Lay motionless: and every battle ship
Stood still; and every ship of merchandise,
And all that sailed, of every name, stood still."
      ROBERT POLLOK: *Course of Time*, Book VII, line 634-647.

II. ENGLISH OF THE EIGHTEENTH CENTURY.

12. *Reign of George III, 1820 back to 1760.—Example written in 1800.*

"There is, it will be confessed, a delicate sensibility to character, a sober desire of reputation, a wish to possess the esteem of the wise and good, felt by the purest minds, which is at the farthest remove from arrogance or vanity. The humility of a noble mind scarcely dares approve of itself, until it has secured the approbation of others. Very different is that restless desire of distinction, that passion for theatrical display, which inflames the heart and occupies the whole attention of vain men. * * * The truly good man is jealous over himself, lest the notoriety of his best actions, by blending itself with their motive, should diminish their value; the vain man performs the same actions for the sake of that notoriety. The good man quietly discharges his duty, and shuns ostentation; the vain man considers every good deed lost that is not publickly displayed. The one is intent upon realities, the other upon semblances: the one aims to *be* virtuous, the other to *appear* so."—ROBERT HALL: *Sermon on Modern Infidelity*.

13. *From Washington's Farewell Address.—Example written in 1796.*

"Of all the dispositions and habits which lead to political prosperity, Religion and Morality are indispensable supports. In vain would that man claim the tribute of patriotism, who should labour to subvert these great pillars of human happiness, these firmest props of the duties of men and citizens. The mere politician, equally with the pious man, ought to respect and cherish them. A volume could not trace all their connexions with private and publick felicity. Let it simply be asked, where is the security for property, for reputation, for life, if the sense of religious obligation desert the oaths which are the instruments of investigation in courts of justice? And let us with caution indulge the supposition, that morality can be maintained without religion. Whatever may be conceded to the influence of refined education on minds of a peculiar structure; reason and experience both forbid us to expect that national morality can prevail in exclusion of religious principle."—GEORGE WASHINGTON.

14. *From Dr. Johnson's Life of Addison.—Example written about 1780.*

"That he always wrote as he would think it necessary to write now, cannot be affirmed; his instructions were such as the character of his readers made proper. That general knowledge which now circulates in common talk, was in his time rarely to be found. Men not professing learning, were not ashamed of ignorance; and in the female world, any acquaintance with books was distinguished only to be censured. His purpose was to infuse literary curiosity, by gentle and unsuspected conveyance, into the gay, the idle, and the wealthy; he therefore presented knowledge in the most alluring form, not lofty and austere, but accessible and familiar. When he shewed them their defects, he shewed them likewise that they might easily be supplied. His attempt succeeded; inquiry was awakened, and comprehension expanded. An emulation of intellectual elegance was excited, and from this time to our own, life has been gradually exalted, and conversation purified and enlarged."—SAMUEL JOHNSON: *Lives*, p. 321.

15. *Reign of George II, 1760 back to 1727.—Example written in 1751.*

"We Britons in our time have been remarkable borrowers, as our *multiform* Language may sufficiently shew. Our Terms in *polite Literature* prove, that this came from *Greece*; our terms in *Music* and *Painting*, that these came from Italy; our Phrases in *Cookery* and *War*, that we learnt these from the French; and our phrases in *Navigation*, that we were taught by the *Flemings* and *Low Dutch*. These many and very different Sources of our Language may be the cause, why it is so deficient in *Regularity* and *Analogy*. Yet we have this advantage to compensate the defect, that what we want in *Elegance*, we gain in *Copiousness*, in which last respect few Languages will be found superior to our own."—JAMES HARRIS: *Hermes*, Book iii, Ch. v, p. 408.

16. *Reign of George I, 1727 back to 1714.—Example written about 1718.*

"There is a certain coldness and indifference in the phrases of our European languages, when they are compared with the Oriental forms of speech: and it happens very luckily, that the Hebrew idioms ran into the English tongue, with a particular grace and beauty. Our language has received innumerable elegancies and improvements from that infusion of Hebraisms, which are derived to it out of the poetical passages in holy writ. They give a force and energy to our expressions, warm and animate our language, and convey our thoughts in more ardent and intense phrases, than any that are to be met with in our tongue."—JOSEPH ADDISON: *Evidences*, p. 192.

17. *Reign of Queen Anne, 1714 to 1702.—Example written in 1708.*

"Some by old words to Fame have made pretence,
Ancients in phrase, mere moderns in their sense;
Such labour'd nothings, in so strange a style,
Amaze th' unlearn'd, and make the learned smile."
"In words, as fashions, the same rule will hold;
Alike fantastick, if too new or old:
Be not the first by whom the new are try'd,
Nor yet the last to lay the old aside."
ALEXANDER POPE: *Essay on Criticism*, l. 324-336.

III. ENGLISH OF THE SEVENTEENTH CENTURY.

18. *Reign of William III, 1702 to 1689.—Example published in 1700.*

"And when we see a Man of *Milton's* Wit *Chime* in with such a *Herd*, and Help on the *Cry* against *Hirelings*! We find How Easie it is for *Folly* and *Knavery* to Meet, and that they are Near of Kin, tho they bear Different Aspects. Therefor since *Milton* has put himself upon a *Level* with the *Quakers* in this, I will let them go together. And take as little Notice of his *Buffoonry*, as of their *Dulness* against *Tythes*. Ther is nothing worth *Quoting* in his *Lampoon* against the *Hirelings*. But what ther is of *Argument* in it, is fully Consider'd in what follows."—CHARLES LESLIE: *Divine Right of Tithes, Pref.*, p. xi.

19. *Reign of James II, 1689 back to 1685.—Example written in 1685.*

"His conversation, wit, and parts,
His knowledge in the noblest useful arts,
 Were such, dead authors could not give;
 But habitudes of those who live;
Who, lighting him, did greater lights receive:
 He drain'd from all, and all they knew;
His apprehension quick, his judgment true:
 That the most learn'd with shame confess
His knowledge more, his reading only less."
   JOHN DRYDEN: *Ode to the Memory of Charles II; Poems*, p. 84.

20. *Reign of Charles II, 1685 to 1660.—Example from a Letter to the Earl of Sunderland, dated,* "Philadelphia, 28th 5th mo. July, 1683."

"And I will venture to say, that by the help of God, and such noble Friends, I will show a Province in seven years, equal to her neighbours of forty years planting. I have lay'd out the Province into Countys. Six are begun to be seated; they lye on the great river, and are planted about six miles back. The town platt is a mile long, and two deep,—has a navigable river on each side, the least as broad as the Thames at Woolwych, from three to eight fathom water. There is built about eighty houses, and I have settled at least three hundred farmes contiguous to it."—WILLIAM PENN. *The Friend*, Vol. vii, p. 179.

21. *From an Address or Dedication to Charles II.—Written in 1675.*

"There is no [other] king in the world, who can so experimentally testify of God's providence and goodness; neither is there any [other], who rules so many free people, so many true Christians: which thing renders thy government more honourable, thyself more considerable, than the accession of many nations filled with slavish and superstitious souls."—ROBERT BARCLAY: *Apology*, p. viii.

22. The following example, from the commencement of *Paradise Lost*, first published in 1667, has been cited by several authors, to show how large a proportion of our language is of Saxon origin. The thirteen words in Italics are the only ones in this passage, which seem to have been derived from any other source.

"Of man's first *disobedience,* and the *fruit*
Of that forbidden tree, whose *mortal* taste
Brought death into the world, and all our woe,
With loss of *Eden*; till one greater Man
Restore us, and *regain* the blissful *seat,*
Sing, heav'nly *Muse,* that on the *secret* top
Of *Oreb,* or of *Sinai,* didst *inspire*
That shepherd, who first taught the chosen seed,
In the beginning, how the Heav'ns and Earth
Rose out of *Chaos.*"—MILTON: *Paradise Lost*, Book I.

23. *Examples written during Cromwell's Protectorate, 1660 to 1650.*

"The Queene was pleased to shew me the letter, the seale beinge a Roman eagle, havinge characters about it almost like the Greeke. This day, in the afternoone, the vice-chauncellor came to me and stayed about four hours with me; in which tyme we conversed upon the longe debates."—WHITELOCKE. *Bucke's Class. Gram.*, p. 149.

"I am yet heere, and have the States of Holland ingaged in a more than ordnary maner, to procure me audience of the States Generall. Whatever happen, the effects must needes be good."—STRICKLAND: *Bucke's Classical Gram.*, p. 149.

24. *Reign of Charles I, 1648 to 1625.—Example from Ben Jonson's Grammar, written about 1634; but the orthography is more modern.*

"The second and third person singular of the present are made of the first, by adding *est* and *eth*; which last is sometimes shortened into *s*. It seemeth to have been poetical licence which first introduced this abbreviation of the third person into use; but our best grammarians have condemned it upon some occasions, though perhaps not to be absolutely banished the common and familiar style."

"The persons plural keep the termination of the first person singular. In former times, till about the reign of Henry the eighth, they were wont to be formed by adding *en*; thus, *loven, sayen, complainen*. But now (whatever is the cause) it hath quite grown out of use, and that other so generally prevailed, that I dare not presume to set this afoot again: albeit (to tell you my opinion) I am persuaded that the lack hereof well considered, will be found a great blemish to our tongue. For seeing *time* and *person* be, as it were, the right and left hand of a verb, what can the maiming bring else, but a lameness to the whole body?"—Book i, Chap. xvi.

25. *Reign of James I, 1625 to 1603.—From an Advertisement, dated 1608.*

"I svppose it altogether needlesse (Christian Reader) by commending M. *VVilliam Perkins,* the Author of this booke, to wooe your holy affection, which either himselfe in his life time by his Christian conversation hath woon in you, or sithence his death, the neuer-dying memorie of his excellent knowledge, his great humilitie, his sound religion, his feruent zeale, his painefull labours, in the Church of God, doe most iustly challenge at your hands: onely in one word, I dare be bold to say of him as in times past *Nazianzen* spake of *Athanasius.* His life was a good definition of a true minister and preacher of the Gospell."—*The Printer to the Reader.*

26. *Examples written about the end of Elizabeth's reign—1603.*

"Some say, That euer 'gainst that season comes
Wherein our Saviour's Birth is celebrated,
The Bird of Dawning singeth all night long;
And then, say they, no Spirit dares walk abroad:
The nights are wholsom, then no Planets strike,
No Fairy takes, nor Witch hath pow'r to charm;
So hallow'd and so gracious is the time."
SHAKSPEARE: *Hamlet.*

"The sea, with such a storme as his bare head
In hell-blacke night indur'd, would haue buoy'd up
And quench'd the stelled fires.
Yet, poore old heart, he holpe the heuens to raine.
If wolues had at thy gate howl'd that sterne time,
Thou shouldst haue said, Good porter, turne the key."
SHAKSPEARE: *Lear.*

IV. ENGLISH OF THE SIXTEENTH CENTURY.

27. *Reign of Elizabeth, 1603 back to 1558.—Example written in 1592.*

"As for the soule, it is no accidentarie qualitie, but a spirituall and inuisible essence or nature, subsisting by it selfe. Which plainely appeares in that the soules of men haue beeing and continuance as well forth of the bodies of men as in the same; and are as wel subiect to torments as the bodie is. And whereas we can and doe put in practise sundrie actions of life, sense, motion, vnderstanding, we doe it onely by the power and vertue of the soule. Hence ariseth the difference betweene the soules of men, and beasts. The soules of men are substances: but the soules of other creatures seeme not to be substances; because they haue no beeing out of the bodies in which they are."—WILLIAM PERKINS: *Theol. Works, folio,* p. 155.

28. *Examples written about the beginning of Elizabeth's reign.—1558.*

"Who can perswade, when treason is aboue reason; and mighte ruleth righte; and it is had for lawfull, whatsoever is lustfull; and commotioners are better than commissioners; and common woe is named common weale?"—SIR JOHN CHEKE. "If a yong jentleman will venture him selfe into the companie of ruffians, it is over great a jeopardie, lest their facions, maners, thoughts, taulke, and dedes, will verie sone be over like."—ROGER ASCHAM.

29. *Reign of Mary the Bigot, 1558 to 1553.—Example written about 1555.*

"And after that Philosophy had spoken these wordes the said companye of the musys poeticall beynge rebukyd and sad, caste downe their countenaunce to the grounde, and by blussyng confessed their shamefastnes, and went out of the dores. But I (that had my syght dull and blynd wyth wepyng, so that I knew not what woman this was hauyng soo great aucthoritie) was amasyd or astonyed, and lokyng downeward, towarde the ground, I began pryvyle to look what thyng she would save ferther."—COLVILLE: *Version from Boëthius: Johnson's Hist. of E. L.*, p. 29.

30. *Example referred by Dr. Johnson to the year 1553.*

"Pronunciation is an apte orderinge bothe of the voyce, countenaunce, and all the whole bodye, accordynge to the worthinea of such woordes and mater as by speache are declared. The vse hereof is suche for anye one that liketh to haue prayse for tellynge his tale in open assemblie, that hauing a good tongue, and a comelye countenaunce, he shal be thought to passe all other that haue not the like vtteraunce: thoughe they have muche better learning."—DR. WILSON: *Johnson's Hist. E. L.*, p. 45.

31. *Reign of Edward VI, 1553 to 1547.—Example written about 1550.*

"Who that will followe the graces manyfolde
Which are in vertue, shall finde auauncement:
Wherefore ye fooles that in your sinne are bolde,
Ensue ye wisdome, and leaue your lewde intent,
Wisdome is the way of men most excellent:
Therefore haue done, and shortly spede your pace,
To quaynt your self and company with grace."
  ALEXANDER BARCLAY: *Johnson's Hist. E. L.*, p. 44.

32. *Reign of Henry VIII, 1547 to 1509.—Example dated 1541.*

"Let hym that is angry euen at the fyrste consyder one of these thinges, that like as he is a man, so is also the other, with whom he is angry, and therefore it is as lefull for the other to be angry, as unto hym: and if he so be, than shall that anger be to hym displeasant, and stere hym more to be angrye."—SIR THOMAS ELLIOTT: *Castel of Helthe.*

33. *Example of the earliest English Blank Verse; written about 1540.*

The supposed author died in 1541, aged 38. The piece from which these lines are taken describes the death of *Zoroas*, an Egyptian astronomer, slain in Alexander's first battle with the Persians.

"The Persians waild such sapience to foregoe;
And very sone the Macedonians wisht
He would have lived; king Alexander selfe
Demde him a man unmete to dye at all;
Who wonne like praise for conquest of his yre,
As for stoute men in field that day subdued,
Who princes taught how to discerne a man,
That in his head so rare a jewel beares;
But over all those same Camenes,[49] those same
Divine Camenes, whose honour he procurde,
As tender parent doth his daughters weale,
Lamented, and for thankes, all that they can,
Do cherish hym deceast, and sett hym free,
From dark oblivion of devouring death."
Probably written by SIR THOMAS WYAT.

34. *A Letter written from prison, with a coal.* The writer, *Sir Thomas More*, whose works, both in prose and verse, were considered models of pure and elegant style, had been Chancellor of England, and the familiar confidant of Henry VIII, by whose order he was beheaded in 1535.

"Myne own good doughter, our Lorde be thanked I am in good helthe of bodye, and in good quiet of minde: and of worldly thynges I no more desyer then I haue. I beseche hym make you all mery in the hope of heauen. And such thynges as I somewhat longed to talke with you all, concerning the worlde to come, our Lorde put theim into your myndes, as I truste he doth and better to by hys holy spirite: who blesse you and preserue you all. Written wyth a cole by your tender louing father, who in hys pore prayers forgetteth none of you all, nor your babes, nor your nources, nor your good husbandes, nor your good husbandes shrewde wyues, nor your fathers shrewde wyfe neither, nor our other frendes. And thus fare ye hartely well for lacke of paper. THOMAS MORE, knight."—*Johnson's Hist. E. Lang.*, p. 42.

35. *From More's Description of Richard III.—Probably written about 1520.*

"Richarde the third sonne, of whom we nowe entreate, was in witte and courage egall with either of them, in bodye and prowesse farre vnder them bothe, little of stature, ill fetured of limmes, croke backed, his left shoulder much higher than his right, hard fauoured of visage, and such as is in states called warlye, in other menne otherwise, he was malicious, wrathfull, enuious, and from afore his birth euer frowarde. * * * Hee was close and secrete, a deep dissimuler, lowlye of counteynaunce, arrogant of heart—dispitious and cruell, not for euill will alway, but after for ambicion, and either for the suretie and encrease of his estate. Frende and foo was muche what indifferent, where his aduauntage grew, he spared no mans deathe, whose life withstoode his purpose. He slew with his owne handes king Henry the sixt, being prisoner in the Tower."—SIR THOMAS MORE: *Johnson's History of the English Language*, p. 39.

36. *From his description of Fortune, written about the year 1500.*

"Fortune is stately, solemne, prowde, and hye:
And rychesse geueth, to haue seruyce therefore.

The nedy begger catcheth an half peny:

Some manne a thousaude pounde, some lesse some more.

But for all that she kepeth euer in store,

From euery manne some parcell of his wyll,

That he may pray therefore and serve her styll.

  Some manne hath good, but chyldren hath he none.

Some manne hath both, but he can get none health.

Some hath al thre, but vp to honours trone,

Can he not crepe, by no maner of stelth.

To some she sendeth chyldren, ryches, welthe,

Honour, woorshyp, and reuerence all hys lyfe:

But yet she pyncheth hym with a shrewde wife."
          SIR THOMAS MORE.

V. ENGLISH OF THE FIFTEENTH CENTURY.

37. *Example for the reign of Henry VII, who was crowned on Bosworth field, 1485, and who died in 1509.*

"Wherefor and forasmoche as we haue sent for our derrest wif, and for our derrest moder, to come unto us, and that we wold have your advis and counsail also in soche matters as we haue to doo for the subduying of the rebelles, we praie you, that, yeving your due attendaunce vppon our said derrest wif and lady moder, ye come with thaym unto us; not failing herof as ye purpose to doo us plaisir. Yeven undre our signett, at our Castell of Kenelworth, the xiii daie of Maye."—HENRY VII: *Letter to the Earl of Ormond: Bucke's Classical Gram.*, p. 147.

38. *Example for the short reign of Richard III,—from 1485 to 1483.*

"Right reverend fader in God, right trusty and right wel-beloved, we grete yow wele, and wol and charge you that under oure greate seale, being in your warde, ye do make in all haist our lettres of proclamation severally to be directed unto the shirrefs of everie countie within this oure royaume."—RICHARD III: *Letter to his Chancellor.*

39. *Reign of Edward IV,—from 1483 to 1461.—Example written in 1463.*

"Forasmoche as we by divers meanes bene credebly enformed and undarstand for certyne, that owr greate adversary Henry, naminge hym selfe kynge of England, by the maliceous counseyle and exitacion of Margaret his wife, namynge hir selfe queane of England, have conspired," &c.— EDWARD IV: *Letter of Privy Seal.*

40. *Examples for the reign of Henry VI,—from 1461 back to 1422.*

"When Nembroth [i.e. *Nimrod*] by Might, for his own Glorye, made and incorporate the first Realme, and subduyd it to hymself by Tyrannye, he would not have it governyd by any other Rule or Lawe, but by his own Will; by which and for th' accomplishment thereof he made it. And therefor, though he had thus made a Realme, holy Scripture denyd to cal hym a Kyng, *Quia Rex dicitur a Regendo*; Whych thyng he did not, but oppressyd the People by Myght."—SIR JOHN FORTESCUE.

41. *Example from Lydgate, a poetical Monk, who died in 1440.*

"Our life here short of wit the great dulnes
The heuy soule troubled with trauayle,
And of memorye the glasyng brotelnes,
Drede and vncunning haue made a strong batail
With werines my spirite to assayle,
And with their subtil creping in most queint

Hath made my spirit in makyng for to feint."
　　JOHN LYDGATE: *Fall of Princes*, Book III, Prol.

42. *Example for the reign of Henry V,—from 1422 back to 1413.*

"I wolle that the Duc of Orliance be kept stille withyn the Castil of Pontefret, with owte goyng to Robertis place, or to any other disport, it is better he lak his disport then we were disceyved. Of all the remanant dothe as ye thenketh."—*Letter of* HENRY V.

43. *Example for the reign of Henry IV,—from 1413 back to 1400.*

"Right heigh and myghty Prynce, my goode and gracious Lorde,—I recommaund me to you as lowly as I kan or may with all my pouer hert, desiryng to hier goode and gracious tydynges of your worshipful astate and welfare."—LORD GREY: *Letter to the Prince of Wales: Bucke's Classical Gram.*, p. 145.

VI. ENGLISH OF THE FOURTEENTH CENTURY.

44. *Reign of Richard II, 1400 back to 1377.—Example written in 1391.* "Lytel Lowys my sonne, I perceve well by certaine evidences thyne abylyte to lerne scyences, touching nombres and proporcions, and also well consydre I thy besye prayer in especyal to lerne the tretyse of the *astrolabye*. Than for as moche as a philosopher saithe, he wrapeth hym in his frende, that condiscendeth to the ryghtfull prayers of his frende: therefore I have given the a sufficient astrolabye for oure orizont, compownded after the latitude of Oxenforde: vpon the whiche by meditacion of this lytell tretise, I purpose to teche the a certame nombre of conclusions, pertainynge to this same instrument."—GEOFFREY CHAUCER: *Of the Astrolabe.*

45. *Example written about 1385—to be compared with that of 1555, on p. 87.*

"And thus this companie of muses iblamed casten wrothly the chere dounward to the yerth, and shewing by rednesse their shame, thei passeden sorowfully the thresholde. And I of whom the sight plounged in teres was darked, so that I ne might not know what that woman was, of so Imperial aucthoritie, I woxe all abashed and stonied, and cast my sight doune to the yerth, and began still for to abide what she would doen afterward."—CHAUCER: *Version from Boëthius: Johnson's Hist. of E. L.*, p. 29.

46. *Poetical Example—probably written before 1380.*

"O Socrates, thou stedfast champion;
She ne might nevir be thy turmentour,
Thou nevir dreddist her oppression,
Ne in her chere foundin thou no favour,
Thou knewe wele the disceipt of her colour,
And that her moste worship is for to lie,
I knowe her eke a false dissimulour,
For finally Fortune I doe defie."—CHAUCER.

47. *Reign of Edward III, 1377 to 1327.—Example written about 1360.*

"And eke full ofte a littell skare
Vpon a banke, er men be ware,
Let in the streme, whiche with gret peine,
If any man it shall restreine.
Where lawe failleth, errour groweth;
He is not wise, who that ne troweth."—SIR JOHN GOWER.

48. *Example from Mandeville, the English traveller—written in 1356.*

"And this sterre that is toward the Northe, that wee clepen the lode sterre, ne apperethe not to hem. For whiche cause, men may wel perceyve, that the lond and the see ben of rownde schapp and forme. For the partie of the firmament schewethe in o contree, that schewethe not in another contree. And men may well preven be experience and sotyle compassement of wytt, that zif a man fond passages be schippes, that wolde go to serchen the world, men mighte go be schippe all aboute the world, and aboven and benethen. The whiche thing I prove thus, aftre that I have seyn. * * * Be the whiche I seye zou certeynly, that men may envirowne alle the erthe of alle the world, as wel undre as aboven, and turnen azen to his contree, that hadde companye and schippynge and conduyt: and alle weyes he scholde fynde men, londes, and yles, als wel as in this contree."—SIR JOHN MANDEVILLE; *Johnson's Hist. of E. L.*, p. 26.

49. *Example from Rob. Langland's "Vision of Pierce Ploughman," 1350.*

"In the somer season,
When hot was the Sun,
I shope me into shroubs,
As I a shepe were;
In habit as an harmet,
Vnholy of werkes,
Went wyde in this world
Wonders to heare."

50. *Description of a Ship—referred to the reign of Edward II: 1327-1307.*

"Such ne saw they never none,
For it was so gay begone,
Every nayle with gold ygrave,
Of pure gold was his sklave,
Her mast was of ivory,

Of samyte her sayle wytly,
Her robes all of whyte sylk,
As whyte as ever was ony mylke.
The noble ship was without
With clothes of gold spread about
And her loft and her wyndlace
All of gold depaynted was."
   ANONYMOUS: *Bucke's Gram.*, p. 143.

51. *From an Elegy on Edward I, who reigned till 1307 from 1272.*

"Thah mi tonge were made of stel,
  Ant min herte yzote of bras,
The goodness myht y never telle,
  That with kyng Edward was:
Kyng, as thou art cleped conquerour,
  In uch battaille thou hadest prys;
God bringe thi soule to the honour,
  That ever wes ant ever ys.
Now is Edward of Carnavan
  Kyng of Engelond al aplyght;
God lete him never be worse man
  Then his fader, ne lasse myht,
To holden his pore men to ryht,
  Ant understonde good counsail,
Al Engelond for to wysse and dyht;
  Of gode knyhtes darh him nout fail."
   ANON.: *Percy's Reliques*, Vol. ii, p. 10.

VII. ENGLISH OF THE THIRTEENTH CENTURY.

52. *Reign of Henry III, 1272 to 1216.—Example from an old ballad entitled Richard of Almaigne*; which Percy says was "made by one of the adherents of Simon de Montfort, earl of Leicester, soon after the battle of Lewes, which was fought, May 14, 1264."—*Percy's Reliques*, Vol. ii.

> "Sitteth alle stille, and herkneth to me;
> The kyng of Almaigne, bi mi leaute,
> Thritti thousent pound askede he
> For te make the pees in the countre,
>   Ant so he dude more.
>   Richard, thah thou be ever trichard,
>   Trichten shalt thou never more."

53. In the following examples, I substitute Roman letters for the Saxon. At this period, we find the characters mixed. The style here is that which Johnson calls "a kind of intermediate diction, neither Saxon nor English." Of these historical rhymes, by *Robert of Gloucester*, the Doctor gives us more than two hundred lines; but he dates them no further than to say, that the author "is placed by the criticks in the thirteenth century."—*Hist. of Eng. Lang.*, p. 24.

> "Alfred thys noble man, as in the ger of grace he nom
> Eygte hondred and syxty and tuelue the kyndom.
> Arst he adde at Rome ybe, and, vor ys grete wysdom,
> The pope Leo hym blessede, tho he thuder com,
> And the kynges croune of hys lond, that in this lond gut ys:
> And he led hym to be kyng, ar he kyng were y wys.
> An he was kyng of Engelond, of alle that ther come,
> That vorst thus ylad was of the pope of Rome,
> An suththe other after hym of the erchebyssopes echon."

> "Clere he was god ynou, and gut, as me telleth me,
> He was more than ten ger old, ar he couthe ys abece.
> Ac ys gode moder ofte smale gyftes hym tok,
> Vor to byleue other pie, and loky on ys boke.
> So that by por clergye ys rygt lawes he wonde,
> That neuere er nere y mad to gouerny ys lond."
>   ROBERT OF GLOUCESTER: *Johnson's Hist. of E. L.*, p. 25.

54. *Reign of John, 1216 back to 1199.*—*Subject of Christ's Crucifixion.*

> "I syke when y singe for sorewe that y se
> When y with wypinge bihold upon the tre,
> Ant se Jhesu the suete ys hert blod for-lete
>   For the love of me;
> Ys woundes waxen wete, thei wepen, still and mete,
>   Marie reweth me."
>   ANON.: *Bucke's Gram.*, p. 142.

VIII. ENGLISH, OR ANGLO-SAXON, OF THE TWELFTH CENTURY.

55. *Reign of Richard I, 1199 back to 1189.*—*Owl and Nightingale.*

> "Ich was in one sumere dale,
> In one snive digele pale,
> I herde ich hold grete tale,
> An hule and one nightingale.
> That plait was stif I stare and strong,
> Sum wile softe I lud among.
> An other again other sval
> I let that wole mod ut al.
> I either seide of otheres custe,
> That alere worste that hi wuste

I hure and I hure of others songe
Hi hold plaidung futhe stronge."
  ANON.: *Bucke's Gram.*, p. 142.

56. *Reign of Henry II, 1189 back to 1154.—Example dated 1180.*

"And of alle than folke
The wuneden ther on folde,
Wes thisses landes folke
Leodene hendest itald;
And alswa the wimmen
Wunliche on heowen."
  GODRIC: *Bucke's Gram.*, p. 141.

57. *Example from the Saxon Chronicle, written about 1160.*

"Micel hadde Henri king gadered gold & syluer, and na god ne dide me for his saule thar of. Tha the king Stephne to Engla-land com, tha macod he his gadering æt Oxene-ford, & thar he nam the biscop Roger of Seres-beri, and Alexander biscop of Lincoln, & te Canceler Roger hife neues, & dide ælle in prisun, til hi jafen up here castles. Tha the suikes undergæton that he milde man was & softe & god, & na justise ne dide; tha diden hi alle wunder." See *Johnson's Hist. of the Eng. Language*, p. 22.

58. *Reign of Stephen, 1154 to 1135.—Example written about this time.*

"Fur in see bi west Spaygne.
Is a lond ihone Cokaygne.
There nis lond under heuenriche.
Of wel of godnis hit iliche.
Thoy paradis be miri and briyt.
Cokaygne is of fairer siyt.

What is ther in paradis.
Bot grasse and flure and greneris.
Thoy ther be ioi and gret dute.
Ther nis met bot ænlic frute.
Ther nis halle bure no bench.
Bot watir manis thurst to quench."
      ANON.: *Johnson's Hist. Eng. Lang.*, p. 23.

59. *Reign of Henry I, 1135 to 1100.—Part of an Anglo-Saxon Hymn*.

"Heuene & erthe & all that is,
  Biloken is on his honde.
He deth al that his wille is,
  On sea and ec on londe.

  He is orde albuten orde.
    And ende albuten ende.
He one is eure on eche stede,
  Wende wer thu wende.

  He is buuen us and binethen,
    Biuoren and ec bihind.
Se man that Godes wille deth,
  He mai hine aihwar uinde.

  Eche rune he iherth,
    And wot eche dede.
He durh sighth eches ithanc,
  Wai hwat sel us to rede.

  Se man neure nele don god,
  Ne neure god lif leden,

Er deth & dom come to his dure,
  He mai him sore adreden.

  Hunger & thurst, hete & chele,
   Ecthe and all unhelthe,
 Durh deth com on this midelard,
   And other uniselthe.

   Ne mai non herte hit ithenche,
   Ne no tunge telle,
 Hu muchele pinum and hu uele,
   Bieth inne helle.

   Louie God mid ure hierte,
   And mid all ure mihte,
  And ure emcristene swo us self,
   Swo us lereth drihte."
        ANON.: *Johnson's Hist. Eng. Lang.*, p. 21.

IX. ANGLO-SAXON OF THE ELEVENTH CENTURY, COMPARED WITH ENGLISH.

60. *Saxon,—11th Century.*[50]

LUCÆ, CAP. I.

"5. On Herodes dagum Iudea cynincges, wæs sum sacred on naman Zacharias, of Abian tune: and his wif wæs of Aarones dohtrum, and hyre nama waas Elizabeth.

6. Sothlice hig wæron butu rihtwise beforan Gode, gangende on eallum his bebodum and rihtwisnessum, butan wrohte.

7. And hig næfdon nan bearn, fortham the Elizabeth wæs unberende; and hy on hyra dagum butu forth-eodun.

8. Sothlice wæs geworden tha Zacharias hys sacerdhades breac on his gewrixles endebyrdnesse beforan Gode,

9. Æfter gewunan thæs sacerdhades hlotes, he eode that he his offrunge sette, tha he on Godes tempel eode.

10. Eall werod thæs folces wæs ute gebiddende on thære offrunge timan.

11. Tha ætywde him Drihtnes engel standende on thæs weofodes swithran healfe.

12. Tha weard Zacharias gedrefed that geseonde, and him ege onhreas.

13. Tha cwæth se engel him to, Ne ondræd thu the Zacharias; fortham thin ben is gehyred, and thin wif Elizabeth the sunu centh, and thu nemst hys naman Johannes."—*Saxon Gospels*.

English.—14th Century.

LUK, CHAP. I.

"5. In the dayes of Eroude kyng of Judee ther was a prest Zacarye by name, of the sort of Abia: and his wyf was of the doughtris of Aaron, and hir name was Elizabeth.

6. And bothe weren juste bifore God, goynge in alle the maundementis and justifyingis of the Lord, withouten playnt.

7. And thei hadden no child, for Elizabeth was bareyn; and bothe weren of greet age in her dayes.

8. And it befel that whanne Zacarye schould do the office of presthod in the ordir of his course to fore God,

9. Aftir the custom of the presthood, he wente forth by lot, and entride into the temple to encensen.

10. And al the multitude of the puple was without forth and preyede in the our of encensying.

11. And an aungel of the Lord apperide to him, and stood on the right half of the auter of encense. 12. And Zacarye seyinge was afrayed, and drede fel upon him.

13. And the aungel sayde to him, Zacarye, drede thou not; for thy preier is herd, and Elizabeth thi wif schal bere to thee a sone, and his name schal be clepid Jon."

Wickliffe's Bible, 1380.

English.—17th Century.

LUKE, CHAP. I.

"5. There was in the days of Herod the king of Judea, a certain priest named Zacharias, of the course of Abia: and his wife was of the daughters of Aaron, and her name was Elisabeth.

6. And they were both righteous before God, walking in all the commandments and ordinances of the Lord, blameless.

7. And they had no child, because that Elisabeth was barren; and they both were now well stricken in years.

8. And it came to pass, that while he executed the priest's office before God in the order of his course,

9. According to the custom of the priest's office, his lot was to burn incense when he went into the temple of the Lord.

10. And the whole multitude of the people were praying without at the time of incense.

11. And there appeared unto him an angel of the Lord, standing on the right side of the altar of incense.

12. And when Zacharias saw him, he was troubled, and fear fell upon him.

13. But the angel said unto him, Fear not, Zacharias; for thy prayer is heard, and thy wife Elisabeth shall bear thee a son, and thou shall call his name John."

Common Bible, 1610.

See Dr. Johnson's History of the English Language, in his Quarto Dictionary.

X. ANGLO-SAXON IN THE TIME OF KING ALFRED.

61. Alfred the Great, who was the youngest son of Ethelwolf, king of the West Saxons, succeeded to the crown on the death of his brother Ethelred, in the year 871, being then twenty-two years old. He had scarcely time to attend the funeral of his brother, before he was called to the field to defend his country against the Danes. After a reign of more than twenty-eight years, rendered singularly glorious by great achievements under difficult

circumstances, he died universally lamented, on the 28th of October, A. D. 900. By this prince the university of Oxford was founded, and provided with able teachers from the continent. His own great proficiency in learning, and his earnest efforts for its promotion, form a striking contrast with the ignorance which prevailed before. "In the ninth century, throughout the whole kingdom of the West Saxons, no man could be found who was scholar enough to instruct the young king Alfred, then a child, even in the first elements of reading: so that he was in his twelfth year before he could name the letters of the alphabet. When that renowned prince ascended the throne, he made it his study to draw his people out of the sloth and stupidity in which they lay; and became, as much by his own example as by the encouragement he gave to learned men, the great restorer of arts in his dominions."—*Life of Bacon.*

62. The language of eulogy must often be taken with some abatement: it does not usually present things in their due proportions. How far the foregoing quotation is true, I will not pretend to say; but what is called "the revival of learning," must not be supposed to have begun at so early a period as that of Alfred. The following is a brief specimen of the language in which that great man wrote; but, printed in Saxon characters, it would appear still less like English.

"On thære tide the Gotan of Siththiu mægthe with Romana rice gewin upahofon. and mith heora cyningum. Rædgota and Eallerica wæron hatne. Romane burig abræcon. and eall Italia rice that is betwux tham muntum and Sicilia tham ealonde in anwald gerehton. and tha ægter tham foresprecenan cyningum Theodric feng to tham ilcan rice se Theodric wæs Amulinga. he wass Cristen. theah he on tham Arrianiscan gedwolan durhwunode. He gehet Romanum his freondscype. swa that hi mostan heora ealdrichta wyrthe beon."—KING ALFRED: *Johnson's Hist. of E. L., 4to Dict.*, p. 17.

CHAPTER VIII.

OF THE GRAMMATICAL STUDY OF THE ENGLISH LANGUAGE.

"Grammatica quid est? ars rectè scribendi rectèque loquendi; poetarum enarrationem continens; omnium Scientiarum fons uberrimus. * * * Nostra ætas parum perita rerum veterum, nimis brevi gyro grammaticum sepsit; at apud antiques olim tantum auctoritatis hic ordo habuit, ut censores essent et judices scriptorum omnium soli grammatici; quos ob id etiam Criticos vocabant."—DESPAUTER. *Præf. ad Synt*, fol. 1.

1. Such is the peculiar power of language, that there is scarcely any subject so trifling, that it may not thereby be plausibly magnified into something great; nor are there many things which cannot be ingeniously disparaged till they shall seem contemptible. Cicero goes further: "Nihil est tam incredibile quod non dicendo fiat probabile;"—"There is nothing so incredible that it may not by the power of language be made probable." The study of grammar has been often overrated, and still oftener injuriously decried. I shall neither join with those who would lessen in the public esteem that general system of doctrines, which from time immemorial has been taught as grammar; nor attempt, either by magnifying its practical results, or by decking it out with my own imaginings, to invest it with any artificial or extraneous importance.

2. I shall not follow the footsteps of *Neef*, who avers that, "Grammar and incongruity are identical things," and who, under pretence of reaching the same end by better means, scornfully rejects as nonsense every thing that others have taught under that name; because I am convinced, that, of all methods of teaching, none goes farther than his, to prove the reproachful assertion true. Nor shall I imitate the declamation of *Cardell*; who, at the commencement of his Essay, recommends the general study of language on earth, from the consideration that, "The faculty of speech is the medium of social bliss for superior intelligences in an eternal world;" [51] and who, when he has exhausted censure in condemning the practical instruction of others, thus lavishes praise, in both his grammars, upon that formless, void, and incomprehensible theory of his own: "This application of words," says he, "in their endless use, by one plain rule, to all things which nouns can name, instead of being the fit subject of blind cavil, *is the most sublime theme presented to the intellect on earth. It is the practical intercourse of the soul at once with its God, and with all parts of his works!*"—*Cardell's Gram.*, 12mo, p. 87; *Gram.*, 18mo, p. 49.

3. Here, indeed, a wide prospect opens before us; but he who traces science, and teaches what is practically useful, must check imagination, and be content with sober truth.

"For apt the mind or fancy is to rove
Uncheck'd, and of her roving is no end."—MILTON.

Restricted within its proper limits, and viewed in its true light, the practical science of grammar has an intrinsic dignity and merit sufficient to throw back upon any man who dares openly assail it, the lasting stigma of folly and self-conceit. It is true, the judgements of men are fallible, and many opinions are liable to be reversed by better knowledge: but what has been long established by the unanimous concurrence of the learned, it can hardly be the part of a wise instructor now to dispute. The literary reformer who, with the last named gentleman, imagines "that the persons to whom the civilized world have looked up to for instruction in language were all wrong alike in the main points," [52] intends no middle course of reformation, and must needs be a man either of great merit, or of little modesty.

4. The English language may now be regarded as the common inheritance of about fifty millions of people; who are at least as highly distinguished for virtue, intelligence, and enterprise, as any other equal portion of the earth's population. All these are more or less interested in the purity, permanency, and right use of that language; inasmuch as it is to be, not only the medium of mental intercourse with others for them and their children, but the vehicle of all they value, in the reversion of ancestral honour, or in the transmission of their own. It is even impertinent, to tell a man of any respectability, that the study of this his native language is an object of great importance and interest: if he does not, from these most obvious considerations, feel it to be so, the suggestion will be less likely to convince him, than to give offence, as conveying an implicit censure.

5. Every person who has any ambition to appear respectable among people of education, whether in conversation, in correspondence, in public speaking, or in print, must be aware of the absolute necessity of a competent knowledge of the language in which he attempts to express his thoughts. Many a ludicrous anecdote is told, of persons venturing to use words of which they did not know the proper application; many a ridiculous blunder has been published to the lasting disgrace of the writer; and so intimately does every man's reputation for sense depend upon his skill in the use of language, that it is scarcely possible to acquire the one without the other. Who can tell how much of his own good or ill success, how much of the favour or disregard with which he himself has been treated, may have

depended upon that skill or deficiency in grammar, of which, as often as he has either spoken or written, he must have afforded a certain and constant evidence.[53]

6. I have before said, that to excel in grammar, is but to know better than others wherein grammatical excellence consists; and, as this excellence, whether in the thing itself, or in him that attains to it, is merely comparative, there seems to be no fixed point of perfection beyond which such learning may not be carried. In speaking or writing to different persons, and on different subjects, it is necessary to vary one's style with great nicety of address; and in nothing does true genius more conspicuously appear, than in the facility with which it adopts the most appropriate expressions, leaving the critic no fault to expose, no word to amend. Such facility of course supposes an intimate knowledge of all words in common use, and also of the principles on which they are to be combined.

7. With a language which we are daily in the practice of hearing, speaking, reading, and writing, we may certainly acquire no inconsiderable acquaintance, without the formal study of its rules. All the true principles of grammar were presumed to be known to the learned, before they were written for the aid of learners; nor have they acquired any independent authority, by being recorded in a book, and denominated grammar. The teaching of them, however, has tended in no small degree to settle and establish the construction of the language, to improve the style of our English writers, and to enable us to ascertain with more clearness the true standard of grammatical purity. He who learns only by rote, may speak the words or phrases which he has thus acquired; and he who has the genius to discern intuitively what is regular and proper, may have further aid from the analogies which he thus discovers; but he who would add to such acquisitions the satisfaction of knowing what is right, must make the principles of language his study.

8. To produce an able and elegant writer, may require something more than a knowledge of grammar rules; yet it is argument enough in favour of those rules, that without a knowledge of them no elegant and able writer is produced. Who that considers the infinite number of phrases which words in their various combinations may form, and the utter impossibility that they should ever be recognized individually for the purposes of instruction and criticism, but must see the absolute necessity of dividing words into classes, and of showing, by general rules of formation and construction, the laws to which custom commonly subjects them, or from which she allows them in particular instances to deviate? Grammar, or the art of writing and speaking, must continue to be learned by some persons; because it is of indispensable use to society. And the only question is, whether children and youth shall acquire it by a regular process of study and method of instruction, or be left to glean it solely from their own occasional observation of the manner in which other people speak and write.

9. The practical solution of this question belongs chiefly to parents and guardians. The opinions of teachers, to whose discretion the decision will sometimes be left, must have a certain degree of influence upon the public mind; and the popular notions of the age, in respect to the relative value of different studies, will doubtless bias many to the adoption or the rejection of this. A consideration of the point seems to be appropriate here, and I cannot forbear to commend the study to the favour of my readers; leaving every one, of course, to choose how much he will be influenced by my advice, example, or arguments. If past experience and the history of education be taken for guides, the study of English grammar will not be neglected; and the method of its inculcation will become an object of particular inquiry and solicitude. The English language ought to be learned at school or in colleges, as other languages usually are; by the study of its grammar, accompanied with regular exercises of parsing, correcting, pointing, and scanning; and by the perusal of some of its most accurate writers,

accompanied with stated exercises in composition and elocution. In books of criticism, our language is already more abundant than any other. Some of the best of these the student should peruse, as soon as he can understand and relish them. Such a course, pursued with regularity and diligence, will be found the most direct way of acquiring an English style at once pure, correct, and elegant.

10. If any intelligent man will represent English grammar otherwise than as one of the most useful branches of study, he may well be suspected of having formed his conceptions of the science, not from what it really is in itself, but from some of those miserable treatises which only caricature the subject, and of which it is rather an advantage to be ignorant. But who is so destitute of good sense as to deny, that a graceful and easy conversation in the private circle, a fluent and agreeable delivery in public speaking, a ready and natural utterance in reading, a pure and elegant style in composition, are accomplishments of a very high order? And yet of all these, the proper study of English grammar is the true foundation. This would never be denied or doubted, if young people did not find, under some other name, better models and more efficient instruction, than what was practised on them for grammar in the school-room. No disciple of an able grammarian can ever speak ill of grammar, unless he belong to that class of knaves who vilify what they despair to reach.

11. By taking proper advantage of the ductility of childhood, intelligent parents and judicious teachers may exercise over the studies, opinions, and habits of youth a strong and salutary control; and it will seldom be found in experience, that those who have been early taught to consider grammatical learning as worthy and manly, will change their opinion in after life. But the study of grammar is not so enticing that it may be disparaged in the hearing of the young, without injury. What would be the natural effect of the following sentence, which I quote from a late well-written religious

homily? "The pedagogue and his dunce may exercise their wits correctly enough, in the way of grammatical analysis, on some splendid argument, or burst of eloquence, or thrilling descant, or poetic rapture, to the strain and soul of which not a fibre in their nature would yield a vibration."—*New-York Observer*, Vol. ix, p. 73.

12. Would not the bright boy who heard this from the lips of his reverend minister, be apt the next day to grow weary of the parsing lesson required by his schoolmaster? And yet what truth is there in the passage? One can no more judge of the fitness of language, without regard to the meaning conveyed by it, than of the fitness of a suit of clothes, without knowing for whom they were intended. The grand clew to the proper application of all syntactical rules, is *the sense*; and as any composition is faulty which does not rightly deliver the author's meaning, so every solution of a word or sentence is necessarily erroneous, in which that meaning is not carefully noticed and literally preserved. To parse rightly and fully, is nothing else than to understand rightly and explain fully; and whatsoever is well expressed, it is a shame either to misunderstand or to misinterpret.

13. This study, when properly conducted and liberally pursued, has an obvious tendency to dignify the whole character. How can he be a man of refined literary taste, who cannot speak and write his native language grammatically? And who will deny that every degree of improvement in literary taste tends to brighten and embellish the whole intellectual nature? The several powers of the mind are not so many distinct and separable agents, which are usually brought into exercise one by one; and even if they were, there might be found, in a judicious prosecution of this study, a healthful employment for them all. The *imagination*, indeed, has nothing to do with the elements of grammar; but in the exercise of composition, young fancy may spread her wings as soon as they are fledged; and for this

exercise the previous course of discipline will have furnished both language and taste, as well as sentiment.

14. The regular grammatical study of our language is a thing of recent origin. Fifty or sixty years ago, such an exercise was scarcely attempted in any of the schools, either in this country or in England.[54] Of this fact we have abundant evidence both from books, and from the testimony of our venerable fathers yet living. How often have these presented this as an apology for their own deficiencies, and endeavoured to excite us to greater diligence, by contrasting our opportunities with theirs! Is there not truth, is there not power, in the appeal? And are we not bound to avail ourselves of the privileges which they have provided, to build upon the foundations which their wisdom has laid, and to carry forward the work of improvement? Institutions can do nothing for us, unless the love of learning preside over and prevail in them. The discipline of our schools can never approach perfection, till those who conduct, and those who frequent them, are strongly actuated by that disposition of mind, which generously aspires to all attainable excellence.

15. To rouse this laudable spirit in the minds of our youth, and to satisfy its demands whenever it appears, ought to be the leading objects with those to whom is committed the important business of instruction. A dull teacher, wasting time in a school-room with a parcel of stupid or indolent boys, knows nothing of the satisfaction either of doing his own duty, or of exciting others to the performance of theirs. He settles down in a regular routine of humdrum exercises, dreading as an inconvenience even such change as proficiency in his pupils must bring on; and is well content to do little good for little money, in a profession which he honours with his services merely to escape starvation. He has, however, one merit: he pleases his patrons, and is perhaps the only man that can; for they must needs be of that class to whom moral restraint is tyranny, disobedience to teachers, as

often right as wrong; and who, dreading the expense, even of a school-book, always judge those things to be cheapest, which cost the least and last the longest. What such a man, or such a neighbourhood, may think of English grammar, I shall not stop to ask.

16. To the following opinion from a writer of great merit, I am inclined to afford room here, because it deserves refutation, and, I am persuaded, is not so well founded as the generality of the doctrines with which it is presented to the public. "Since human knowledge is so much more extensive than the opportunity of individuals for acquiring it, it becomes of the greatest importance so to economize the opportunity as to make it subservient to the acquisition of as large and as valuable a portion as we can. It is not enough to show that a given branch of education is useful: you must show that it is the most useful that can be selected. Remembering this, I think it would be expedient to dispense with the formal study of English grammar,—a proposition which I doubt not many a teacher will hear with wonder and disapprobation. We learn the grammar in order that we may learn English; and we learn English whether we study grammars or not. Especially we *shall* acquire a competent knowledge of our own language, if other departments of our education were improved."

17. "A boy learns more English grammar by joining in an hour's conversation with educated people, than in poring for an hour over Murray or Horne Tooke. If he is accustomed to such society and to the perusal of well-written books, he will learn English grammar, though he never sees a word about syntax; and if he is not accustomed to such society and such reading, the 'grammar books' at a boarding-school will not teach it. Men learn their own language by habit, and not by rules: and this is just what we might expect; for the grammar of a language is itself formed from the prevalent habits of speech and writing. A compiler of grammar first observes these habits, and then makes his rules: but if a person is himself

familiar with the habits, why study the rules? I say nothing of grammar as a general science; because, although the philosophy of language be a valuable branch of human knowledge, it were idle to expect that school-boys should understand it. The objection is, to the system of attempting to teach children formally that which they will learn practically without teaching."—JONATHAN DYMOND: *Essays on Morality*, p. 195.

18. This opinion, proceeding from a man who has written upon human affairs with so much ability and practical good sense, is perhaps entitled to as much respect as any that has ever been urged against the study in question. And so far as the objection bears upon those defective methods of instruction which experience has shown to be inefficient, or of little use, I am in no wise concerned to remove it. The reader of this treatise will find their faults not only admitted, but to a great extent purposely exposed; while an attempt is here made, as well as in my earlier grammars, to introduce a method which it is hoped will better reach the end proposed. But it may easily be perceived that this author's proposition to dispense with the formal study of English grammar is founded upon an untenable assumption. Whatever may be the advantages of those purer habits of speech, which the young naturally acquire from conversation with educated people, it is not true, that, without instruction directed to this end, they will of themselves become so well educated as to speak and write grammatically. Their language may indeed be comparatively accurate and genteel, because it is learned of those who have paid some attention to the study; but, as they cannot always be preserved from hearing vulgar and improper phraseology, or from seeing it in books, they cannot otherwise be guarded from improprieties of diction, than by a knowledge of the rules of grammar. One might easily back this position by the citation of some scores of faulty sentences from the pen of this very able writer himself.

19. I imagine there can be no mistake in the opinion, that in exact proportion as the rules of grammar are unknown or neglected in any country, will corruptions and improprieties of language be there multiplied. The "general science" of grammar, or "the philosophy of language," the author seems to exempt, and in some sort to commend; and at the same time his proposition of exclusion is applied not merely to the school-grammars, but *a fortiori* to this science, under the notion that it is unintelligible to school-boys. But why should any principle of grammar be the less intelligible on account of the extent of its application? Will a boy pretend that he cannot understand a rule of English grammar, because he is told that it holds good in all languages? Ancient etymologies, and other facts in literary history, must be taken by the young upon the credit of him who states them; but the doctrines of general grammar are to the learner the easiest and the most important principles of the science. And I know of nothing in the true philosophy of language, which, by proper definitions and examples, may not be made as intelligible to a boy, as are the principles of most other sciences. The difficulty of instructing youth in any thing that pertains to language, lies not so much in the fact that its philosophy is above their comprehension, as in our own ignorance of certain parts of so vast an inquiry;—in the great multiplicity of verbal signs; the frequent contrariety of practice; the inadequacy of memory; the inveteracy of ill habits; and the little interest that is felt when we speak merely of words.

20. The grammatical study of our language was early and strongly recommended by Locke,[55] and other writers on education, whose character gave additional weight to an opinion which they enforced by the clearest arguments. But either for want of a good grammar, or for lack of teachers skilled in the subject and sensible of its importance, the general neglect so long complained of as a grievous imperfection in our methods of education, has been but recently and partially obviated. "The attainment of a correct and elegant style," says Dr. Blair, "is an object which demands

application and labour. If any imagine they can catch it merely by the ear, or acquire it by the slight perusal of some of our good authors, they will find themselves much disappointed. The many errors, even in point of grammar, the many offences against purity of language, which are committed by writers who are far from being contemptible, demonstrate, that a *careful study* of the language is previously requisite, in all who aim at writing it properly."—*Blair's Rhetoric,* Lect. ix, p. 91.

21. "To think justly, to write well, to speak agreeably, are the three great ends of academic instruction. The Universities will excuse me, if I observe, that both are, in one respect or other, defective in these three capital points of education. While in Cambridge the general application is turned altogether on speculative knowledge, with little regard to polite letters, taste, or style; in Oxford the whole attention is directed towards classical correctness, without any sound foundation laid in severe reasoning and philosophy. In Cambridge and in Oxford, the art of speaking agreeably is so far from being taught, that it is hardly talked or thought of. *These defects* naturally produce dry unaffecting compositions in the one; superficial taste and puerile elegance in the other; ungracious or affected speech in both."—DR. BROWN, 1757: *Estimate,* Vol. ii, p. 44.

22. "A grammatical study of our own language makes no part of the ordinary method of instruction, which we pass through in our childhood; and it is very seldom we apply ourselves to it afterward. Yet the want of it will not be effectually supplied by any other advantages whatsoever. Much practice in the polite world, and a general acquaintance with the best authors, are good helps; but alone [they] will hardly be sufficient: We have writers, who have enjoyed these advantages in their full extent, and yet cannot be recommended as models of an accurate style. Much less then will, what is commonly called learning, serve the purpose; that is, a critical knowledge of ancient languages, and much reading of ancient authors: The

greatest critic and most able grammarian of the last age, when he came to apply his learning and criticism to an English author, was frequently at a loss in matters of ordinary use and common construction in his own vernacular idiom."—DR. LOWTH, 1763: *Pref. to Gram.*, p. vi.

23. "To the pupils of our public schools the acquisition of their own language, whenever it is undertaken, is an easy task. For he who is acquainted with several grammars already, finds no difficulty in adding one more to the number. And this, no doubt, is one of the reasons why English engages so small a proportion of their time and attention. It is not frequently read, and is still less frequently written. Its supposed facility, however, or some other cause, seems to have drawn upon it such a degree of neglect as certainly cannot be praised. The students in those schools are often distinguished by their compositions in the learned languages, before they can speak or write their own with correctness, elegance, or fluency. A classical scholar too often has his English style to form, when he should communicate his acquisitions to the world. In some instances it is never formed with success; and the defects of his expression either deter him from appearing before the public at all, or at least counteract in a great degree the influence of his work, and bring ridicule upon the author. Surely these evils might easily be prevented or diminished."—DR. BARROW: *Essays on Education*, London, 1804; Philad., 1825, p. 87.

24. "It is also said that those who know Latin and Greek generally express themselves with more clearness than those who do not receive a liberal education. It is indeed natural that those who cultivate their mental powers, write with more clearness than the uncultivated individual. The mental cultivation, however, may take place in the mother tongue as well as in Latin or Greek. Yet the spirit of the ancient languages, further is declared to be superior to that of the modern. I allow this to be the case; but I do not find that the English style is improved by learning Greek. It is known that

literal translations are miserably bad, and yet young scholars are taught to translate, word for word, faithful to their dictionaries. Hence those who do not make a peculiar study of their own language, will not improve in it by learning, in this manner, Greek and Latin. Is it not a pity to hear, what I have been told by the managers of one of the first institutions of Ireland, that it was easier to find ten teachers for Latin and Greek, than one for the English language, though they proposed double the salary to the latter? Who can assure us that the Greek orators acquired their superiority by their acquaintance with foreign languages; or, is it not obvious, on the other hand, that they learned ideas and expressed them in their mother tongue?"—DR. SPURZHEIM: *Treatise on Education*, 1832, p. 107.

25. "Dictionaries were compiled, which comprised all the words, together with their several definitions, or the sense each one expresses and conveys to the mind. These words were analyzed and classed according to their essence, attributes, and functions. Grammar was made a rudiment leading to the principles of all thoughts, and teaching by simple examples, the general classification of words and their subdivisions in expressing the various conceptions of the mind. Grammar is then the key to the perfect understanding of languages; without which we are left to wander all our lives in an intricate labyrinth, without being able to trace back again any part of our way."—*Chazotte's Essay on the Teaching of Languages*, p. 45. Again: "Had it not been for his dictionary and his grammar, which taught him the essence of all languages, and the natural subdivision of their component parts, he might have spent a life as long as Methuselah's, in learning words, without being able to attain to a degree of perfection in any of the languages."—*Ib.*, p. 50. "Indeed, it is not easy to say, to what degree, and in how many different ways, both memory and judgement may be improved by an intimate acquaintance with grammar; which is therefore, with good reason, made the first and fundamental part of literary education. The greatest orators, the most elegant scholars, and the most accomplished

men of business, that have appeared in the world, of whom I need only mention Cæsar and Cicero, were not only studious of grammar, but most learned grammarians."—DR. BEATTIE: *Moral Science,* Vol. i, p. 107.

26. Here, as in many other parts of my work, I have chosen to be liberal of quotations; not to show my reading, or to save the labour of composition, but to give the reader the satisfaction of some other authority than my own. In commending the study of English grammar, I do not mean to discountenance that degree of attention which in this country is paid to other languages; but merely to use my feeble influence to carry forward a work of improvement, which, in my opinion, has been wisely begun, but not sufficiently sustained. In consequence of this improvement, the study of grammar, which was once prosecuted chiefly through the medium of the dead languages, and was regarded as the proper business of those only who were to be instructed in Latin and Greek, is now thought to be an appropriate exercise for children in elementary schools. And the sentiment is now generally admitted, that even those who are afterwards to learn other languages, may best acquire a knowledge of the common principles of speech from the grammar of their vernacular tongue. This opinion appears to be confirmed by that experience which is at once the most satisfactory proof of what is feasible, and the only proper test of what is useful.

27. It must, however, be confessed, that an acquaintance with ancient and foreign literature is absolutely necessary for him who would become a thorough philologist or an accomplished scholar; and that the Latin language, the source of several of the modern tongues of Europe, being remarkably regular in its inflections and systematic in its construction, is in itself the most complete exemplar of the structure of speech, and the best foundation for the study of grammar in general.

www.ingramcontent.com/pod-product-compliance
Lightning Source LLC
Chambersburg PA
CBHW081112080526
44587CB00021B/3552